THE
MAD
MISCELLANY

THE

MAD

MISCELLANY

Terry Deary ✸ Martin Brown

SCHOLASTIC
PRESS

For Sara. TD

To Lisa Edwards, for all the long/short phone calls.
Thanks always. MB

Scholastic Children's Books,
Commonwealth House, 1–19 New Oxford Street,
London WC1A 1NU, UK

A division of Scholastic Ltd
London ~ New York ~ Toronto ~ Sydney ~ Auckland
Mexico City ~ New Delhi ~ Hong Kong

Published in the UK by Scholastic Ltd, 2004

Text copyright © Terry Deary, 2004
Illustrations copyright © Martin Brown, 2004

ISBN 0 439 96803 8

Printed and bound by Scandbook AB, Sweden

2 4 6 8 10 9 7 5 3 1

The right of Terry Deary and Martin Brown to be identified as the author and
illustrator of this work respectively has been asserted by them in accordance with the
Copyright, Designs and Patents Act, 1988.

CONTENTS

INTRODUCTION

Someone once said, 'My family love Horrible Histories books. We always have half a dozen in the toilet.'

Charming. Do they read them? Or do they keep them there in case they run out of toilet paper[1]?

Well here is a special book for people who just want to dip in when they have a few spare moments. You don't HAVE to be on the toilet to do this – but if you are, don't forget to wash your hands after you've touched this book.

You could be on a bus, on a train or on a camel; you could be in the bath, in a boring history lesson or insane. You could be at a football match, at a public execution or at a loose end[2]. Whatever you are, or wherever you are, this is the Horrible Histories book for you.

If you are one of those sad people who has never read a Horrible Histories book before, then you should follow the following warnings carefully:

✘ Do NOT read this if the thought of gushing blood/guts/snot makes you sick. If you ARE brave enough to read this book, then make sure you have a bucket by your side.

✘ Do NOT read this book in the dark with the lights switched off.

✘ Do NOT lend this book to anyone – they may die of horror and sue you.

1. If you are one of those foul families, then perhaps you can answer this question. Just write your answer on the back of a £100 note and send it to the author.
2. If you are at a loose end, please make sure it doesn't drop off.

Apart from that, read and learn some fascinatingly foul facts and incredibly interesting items. There are some things in this book you never knew – and many things you never wanted to know.

So don't whinge that you weren't warned:

HORRIBLE HISTORIES CAN DAMAGE YOUR BRAIN CELL.

 # AWFUL FOR ANIMALS

Have you noticed that hardly anyone writes histories of animals? But big, bad, biting beasts deserve a mention in a Horrible Histories book, don't they?

When humans go to war, dogs go to war. They have become heroes by showing bravery under fire and saving lives (often by giving up their own lives), and there have been some fiercely fighting, murderous mutts too.

――――――― DID YOU KNOW... ―――――――

❀ Attila the Hun (406–453) used giant Molossian dogs (like mastiffs) and talbots (early bloodhounds) in his wars.

❀ His enemies, the Romans, had entire packs of attack dogs, dressed in armour or spiked collars and sent into battle.

❀ During the Middle Ages, armoured war dogs were still being used to defend army camps.

❀ Dogs helped the Spaniards conquer the Indians of Mexico and Peru in the Seven Years War (1756–1763).

❀ Russian dogs were used as messengers by the army of Frederick the Great (1740–1786).

🐾 In the early part of the fourteenth century, the French Navy started to use attack dogs in St Malo, France, to guard naval docks. These were used up to 1770, when they were banned after a young naval officer was killed by one of his own dogs. Oooops!
🐾 The first American Dog Troop was during the Seminole War of 1835, when Cuban bloodhounds were used by the army to track the Indians and runaway slaves in the swamps!

———————— TOP DOGS ————————

Here are the master mutts – the top doggy pets of all time…

Name	Owner	Fact
Peritas	Alexander the Great (356–323 BC)	The all-conquering ancient Greek King named a city after his dog. (Would you like to live in a city called 'Butch'?)
Mathe	Richard II (1367–1400)	Mathe is said to have deserted Richard and switched sides to Henry IV, the man who took his crown. Henry got the throne – Mathe got the bone.
Dragon	Aubry of Montdidier (d. 1371)	Aubry was murdered by a man called Macaire. The French King called for a fight to the death between Macaire (armed with a wooden club) and Aubry's dog. The dog won. Ruff justice.
Boy	Prince Rupert (1619–1682)	At the Battle of Marston Moor in 1644 Rupert forgot to tie up his pet and he ran on to the battlefield. Boy, the bonehead, was killed by a Roundhead.
Pompey	William the Silent (1533–1584)	Pompey woke up William (a Dutch lord) and saved him from an assassination attempt. Did he say 'Thanks' – or stay 'silent'?

Fortune	Josephine de Beauharnais (1763–1814)	Fortune carried secret messages to Napoleon when his wife Josephine was imprisoned. The dog slept at the foot of Josephine's bed and bit Napoleon on the calf on their wedding night. Fangs a lot, Fortune.
Bobbie	Sergeant P Kelly	Bobbie was awarded a medal by Queen Victoria. He survived the Battle of Maiwand (Afghanistan) in 1880, but his master was killed. Bobbie was run over and killed by a cab in London. Taxi one minute – taxidermist the next. Stuffed in a museum now.
Bounce	Admiral Collingwood (1748–1810)	Bounce was aboard the Admiral's ship at the Battle of Trafalgar (1805). Bounce fell overboard and was drowned in 1809. Or was he pushed by the ship's cat?
Greyfriars Bobby	John Gray (d. 1858)	The Skye terrier hung around the Edinburgh tomb of his dead master. People said, 'Ahhhh! Loyal chap,' and fed him. They even gave him his own Greyfriars grave when he finally turned up his tail on 14 January 1872.
Laika	Russian Space Mission, 1957	Laika became the first dog in space when sent up by Russians on *Sputnik 2*. He was put to sleep after nine days, as no plans for safe re-entry had been made. A dog's life.

AN ELEPHANT SOMETIMES FORGETS

Tsar Ivan the Terrible brought the first-ever elephant to Russia. He was told it could bow in front of a mighty man like himself. But when the elephant was taken to the Kremlin Palace, thousands of excited people gathered round. The elephant was terrified. When Ivan appeared, the elephant stood still and seemed to forget how to do its bow.

Ivan was furious. He ordered his soldiers, 'Cut it to pieces!' And that's just what they did. They hacked it into a thousand little bits.

Not a lot of animals know...

The very first bomb dropped on Berlin during World War II killed the only elephant in Berlin Zoo.

 # GRUESOME GAMES

The Romans enjoyed watching people fight – fight each other to the death, or fight animals. Lots of action. Lots of blood. Lots of pain. But they also liked a bit of a change – two men with swords and shields all the time would be boring. So the weapons and the fights chopped and changed – while the fighters just chopped and dropped.

Here are the main types of gladiators. Learn their Latin names and impress your friends!

——— GLORIOUS GLADIATORS ———

Gladiators were always dressed up to look like barbarian warriors … whether they really were barbarians or not[3]. This made the Roman audience feel good. They could watch the slaughters and say, 'Look at those funny men out there – aren't we lucky we are Romans and not like them? OUR soldiers dress in nice little skirts!'

---

3. The Romans said that EVERYONE who wasn't a Roman was a 'barbarian'. They thought anyone who spoke a foreign language sounded as if they were saying, 'Baa-baa-baa-baa' so they were baa-baa-barians … barbarians, geddit?

Andabatae
- short sword
- visored helmet with no eye holes, mail armour for limbs, chest and back plate

Dimachaerus
- two swords

Equestrian
- spear, sword
- helmet, full tunic with arm guard, shield

Hoplomachus
- spear, sword
- large helmet, round shield, complete suit of armour

Laquearius
- noose
- helmet, arm guards, leg guards

Murmillo
- sword
- visored helmet with crest, oblong shield, arm, shoulder and leg guards

Paegniarius
- whip, club
- shield

Provocator
- sword
- visored helmet, curved shield, breastplate, arm and leg guards

Retiarius
- trident, net
- shoulder plate, arm guard

Samnite
- sword
- crested helmet with visor and plume, rectangular shield, arm and leg guards

Secutor
- sword
- round helmet with eye holes, oblong shield, arm and leg guards

Thracian
- curved short sword
- broad-rimmed helmet, small square shield, arm and leg guards

Key ⟸ Weapon ⟐ Armour

PUTRID PIRATES

Many people see pirates as jolly blokes, yo-ho-ho and a bottle of rum. They think of little pirate ships robbing huge Spanish galleons – a bit like Robin Hoods on ships.

The truth is they were ruthless and savage, and spent more time stealing cloth and sugar. What other 'facts' about pirates do most people know?

Have a look at the list. Are the 'facts' true 'always', 'sometimes', or 'never'?

Pirates ... were gentlemen thieves

Answer: Sometimes. Blackbeard was thought to be a 'learned' man born into a well-to-do family. Henry Morgan was made 'Sir Henry' by King Charles II and went on to be Governor of Jamaica. But some were not even men! Mary Read and Anne Bonny were a couple of tough women who swashed and buckled alongside the men.

Pirates ... carried parrots

Answer: Sometimes. The parrots were captured in South America and carried back home. But they weren't just cute pets – they could be sold for good money in Europe. Pretty Polly made a pretty penny.

Pirates ... stole Spanish gold and jewels

Answer: Sometimes. But the Spanish ships became too big and too well armed. Pirates turned to stealing things they could sell – sugar and cloth were popular; slaves made a good price. Never mind the misery.

Pirates ... made maps of buried treasure

Answer: Never. They shared the money and spent it quickly. There was no point in burying it. Captain Kidd was supposed to have buried treasure – but no one has ever found it. It's a daft thing to do with your loot, when you think about it.

Pirates ... wore fine clothes, black beards and curly wigs

Answer: Sometimes. They liked to steal fine clothes from their victims and, if they fitted, they wore them. But pirates like Blackbeard grew a long tangled beard just to look scary. It looked less scary when his head was lopped off in a fight with the British Navy though.

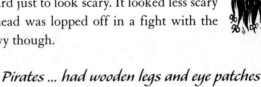

Pirates ... had wooden legs and eye patches

Answer: Sometimes. Cannon shots could mangle legs and smash faces. A saw would take off a crushed leg and there was always wood to make a handy new stump – if stinking gangrene in the wound didn't kill you first.

Pirates ... made enemies walk the plank

Answer: Never. That was just for stories. Pirates never wasted their time. If they wanted an enemy dead, they just chopped them to pieces and fed them to the sharks.

Pirates ... met a crocodile that had swallowed a clock

Answer: Never. Only in the play *Peter Pan*. (And that's not a true story. Pirates never fought with fairies ... I think.)

Pirates ... flew skull-and-cross-bone flags

Answer: Sometimes. But flags often had bleeding hearts or daggers or whole skeletons on them (see below). Black Barty designed his own flag, portraying a giant figure of himself standing, sword in hand, astride two skulls labelled ABH ('A Barbadian's Head') and AMH ('A Martinican's Head').

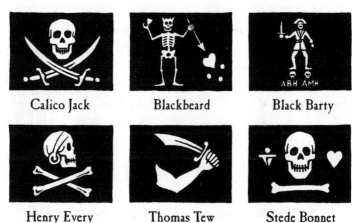

Calico Jack	Blackbeard	Black Barty

Henry Every	Thomas Tew	Stede Bonnet

Pirates ... marooned shipmates on desert islands

Answer: Sometimes. It was a punishment for pirates who broke the rules. Believe it or not, pirates did have a set of rules – just like school rules! The rules even said what time you had to put your lights out and go to bed!

Not a lot of pirates know...

The last person hanged in the US for being a pirate was Captain Nathaniel Gordon, in New York City on 8 March 1862. Gordon had been smuggling slaves into the country.

THE PIRATE RULES

1 Every man on the crew has an equal vote on their action and an equal share of food and drink on the ship. The Captain shall receive two persons' share of any treasure.

2 All men shall have an equal share of treasure. Any man who takes more than his share of gold or jewels or money shall be punished by marooning.[4]

3 No person shall play cards or dice for money.

4 Lights and candles shall be put out at eight o'clock each night.

5 Each person must make sure his own pistol and cutlass are well kept and ready for use at all times.

6 No boy or woman shall be allowed on board the ship when she sails. Any man carrying a woman to sea shall suffer death.

7 Any person who deserts the ship in a battle shall suffer death or marooning.

8 There shall be no fighting on board ship. All quarrels shall be settled on the shore with sword and cutlass.

9 No person shall talk of leaving the crew until everyone has shared at least a thousand pounds.

10 The ship's musicians shall be allowed to rest on a Sunday.

4. Abandoning on an island.

WELL, I'LL BE HANGED

What sort of crimes could you be hanged for in Britain? Here are seven swinging crimes...

Date of law	Crime
1650	Bigamy (getting married when you already have a wife or husband)
1671	Lying in wait with a plan to smash someone's nose
1699	Stealing from a shop anything worth more than 5 shillings (25p)
1723	Poaching, sheep-stealing
1782	Being in the company of gypsies
1810	Horse-stealing, forgery, putting on a disguise, stealing
1816	Begging

Not a lot of criminals know...

There's an old saying, 'If you want to know the time, ask a policeman.' But this has nothing to do with policemen being useful know-it-alls. It's because in the past, policemen were known to find drunks on the street – and pinch their watches as they dozed in the gutter!

ARTFUL ASSASSINS

Peasants (like you and me) could be killed and it would be called 'murder'. But if you are a posh person (someone important, like a potty prime minister or a mad monarch) and you are killed then you are not 'murdered' – you are 'assassinated'.

You are still as dead as a duck's toenail, but 'assassinated' makes you sound more important.

Here are a top ten of topped toffs… Don't try these at home.

Who	When	Awful end
Philip II, King of Macedonia	336 BC	Stabbed by his bodyguard while celebrating his daughter's wedding. Some people have thought that his famous son Alexander the Great might have had something to do with it…
Edmund, King of England	AD 870	Viking raiders captured Edmund. The King wanted to make peace – the Vikings didn't. They tied him to a tree and filled him full of arrows – but didn't kill him. Then they turned him round, cut open his back and pulled his lungs out. Then (just to make sure) they lopped off his head.
St Thomas à Becket, Archbishop of Canterbury	Christmas Day 1170	Butchered at the altar of Canterbury Cathedral. The Archbishop had made himself unpopular with King Henry II, who sent the assassins. Henry later felt sorry – so that's all right.
James I, King of Scotland	1437	Stabbed 28 times in his bedroom. Said to have tried escaping down a drain in the floor, forgetting that he'd had it blocked to stop his tennis balls accidentally rolling down. No more games, James.

Who	When	Awful end
Jean-Paul Marat, French Revolution leader	13 July 1793	Stabbed to death by Charlotte Corday while having a bath. For her crime she was sent to the guillotine, where the executioner snatched her dead head and punched it in the face.

Spencer Perceval, British Prime Minister	11 May 1812	The only British Prime Minister to be assassinated, he was shot dead in the House of Commons by Henry Bellingham, who blamed the Prime Minister for his money problems. Many Brits had parties to celebrate. Bellingham was hanged within a week as crowds cheered, 'God bless you!'
Abraham Lincoln, US President	1862	John Wilkes Booth, an actor, shot Lincoln in Ford's Theatre as he watched a play. Lincoln was guarded by one policeman who sat outside the door. The man got bored and went off for a drink. The assassin simply walked in, placed a pistol to Lincoln's head and pulled the trigger. Booth was later shot dead.(See page 27)
Grigori Rasputin, Russian mad monk and Tsar Nicholas II's pal	31 December 1916	Was fed poisoned cakes AND poisoned wine AND shot in chest AND beaten over head with dumbbell AND tied up AND thrown in icy river. Rasputin had made himself unpopular by getting too friendly with the royal family, especially Tsarina Alexandra.

Franz Ferdinand, Austrian archduke	28 June 1914	Shot in the neck while being driven through Sarajevo in Bosnia. He'd narrowly escaped an assassination attempt earlier that day, when a grenade was thrown at his car, but it hit the one behind. His assassination is said to have started the First World War.
Leon Trotsky, Russian Communist leader	20 August 1940	Ice pick driven through his skull. Trotsky's old friend Joe Stalin had driven Trotsky into exile in Mexico. There he was assassinated by a Stalinist killer, Ramon Mercader, who got 20 years in jail, then went free.

ASSASSINATION AWARDS

Most useful assassination
James Garfield, US President, 2 July 1881. Shot in the back (died 19 September). The doctors poked around to find the bullet and just infected the wound. The bullet didn't kill Garfield – the infection did. US inventor Alexander Graham Bell invented the metal detector so they could do better next time – the invention didn't help Garfield but has made treasure hunters many fortunes over the years.

Weirdest assassination
Georgi Markov, Bulgarian rebel, 7 September 1978. Markov was jabbed with a poison-tipped umbrella on Waterloo Bridge in London. Russian spies were thought to be the brolly assassins. They used the deadly poison ricin.

Unluckiest victim of an assassin
King Henry IV of France, 14 May 1610. Was assassinated by a mad monk, Francois Ravaillac. The unlucky king was caught in a traffic jam so the murdering monk jumped on his carriage and stabbed him twice in the chest. Henry cried, 'I've been stabbed!' then died. The victim of a traffic jam – and a knife, of course.

The only recorded case of an assassinating ape

King Konstantinos of Greece, 1920. King Kon had only one friend, his pet dog. So when the dog was attacked by monkeys, brave King Kon rushed to his rescue. The monkeys bit the King, the wound became infected and the King died in agony of blood poisoning. The dog survived.

Man most often assassinated

Julius Caesar, the Roman leader, 44 BC. Was stabbed to death by 23 assassins. His gory death has been acted out over and over again in Shakespeare's play *Julius Caesar*.

Deadliest doctor assassin

Claudius, Roman Emperor, AD 54. His wife gave him poisoned mushrooms and he fell ill. The doctor told him vomiting would cure the food poisoning. To help, the doctor tickled the Emperor's throat with a feather. The feather was poisoned and finished Claudius off.

Most helpful assassination victim

Alexander II, Tsar of Russia, 1881. Freedom fighters attacked his carriage. A bomb wrapped in newspaper was thrown in front of it, killing the horses and two guards. Alex got out to see how they were. A man called, 'Are you all right?'

Alex said, 'Yes … thank God.'

So the man threw a second bomb, which tore holes in Alex's legs and chest.

Alex said to his guards, 'Take me home to the palace to die.' They did … then Alex did, a few hours later.

The funniest assassination

Count of Rochefoucaulde, 1571. The Count was wakened by a gang of masked men at his bedside. He was sure it was his friends playing a little joke. 'No! Please don't tickle me,' he giggled. 'You know I hate being tickled!' They didn't tickle him. They hacked the cackling Count to death.

Smelliest assassination

King Edmund Ironside, 1016. When Edmund went to the toilet – just a hole in the ground outside the door – little did he know that an assassin was hiding at the bottom of the pit. As the King sat down, the assassin struck up – with a dagger. King Ed, dead.

Mystery assassination

King Charles XII of Sweden, 1718. Charles was not a popular man. When he invaded Norway he was shot dead … but no one can agree on who did it! Was it an enemy bullet? Or one of his own soldiers? His skull is still on show in Stockholm, complete with the bullet hole. But whodunnit?

ABYSMAL ASSASSINS

Of course, some really unlucky leaders suffer from abysmal assassins – killers who botch the job. There have been some fabulous failures over the years.

Here are just ten...

Name of target	Position	Date	Failed assassin
James I and VI	King of England and Scotland (1566–1625)	1605	*Guy Fawkes*. Planned to blow up the King in Parliament. Arrested on 4 November, tortured and executed by hanging, being cut open and chopped into quarters. Guy dummies now burn every 5 November in Britain.
Louis XV	King of France (1710–1774)	1757	*Robert Damiens* (known as 'Robert the Devil') stabbed Louis with a penknife, but Louis didn't die. Punished by having his flesh nipped with red-hot pincers, then being scalded with boiling oil, and finally having his ankles and wrists tied to four horses that pulled him apart.
Andrew Jackson	US President (1767–1845)	30 January, 1835	*Richard Lawrence*. (Claimed to be heir to throne of Britain.) Shot at Jackson in Washington with two pistols, but both misfired. (Odds of that happening have been put at 125,000 to one.)
Louis Philippe	King of France (1773–1850)	1835	*Guiseppe Fiesci* rigged up a machine to fire 25 pistols all at once. As King Louis Philippe went to inspect his troops, Fiesci fired the world's first machine-gun and killed 18 people. But he missed his target, the King! Fiesci went to the guillotine: the executioner didn't miss.

Name of target	Position	Date	Failed assassin
Umberto	King of Italy (1844–1900)	1898	*Luigi Lucchini*. Planned to kill the King for being 'an enemy of the working people' but he could not afford the 50-lire fare to Rome, so he stabbed Elizabeth of Austria instead, even though she'd done nothing to deserve it. Luigi was sentenced to hard labour but hung himself in 1910.
Theodore Roosevelt	Had been US President (1858–1919)	14 October 1912	*John F Schrank*. Shot Theo as he gave a speech. Theo insisted on finishing the speech despite a bullet being lodged in his chest. He was saved by the 50 pages of notes he'd written and stuffed in his pocket.
Franklin D Roosevelt	Later to be US President (1882–1945)	13 November 1933	*Guiseppe Zangara*, who blamed Roosevelt for the pains in his stomach. Fired five shots at him but missed and killed the mayor of Chicago instead. That's bad shooting. Executed on the electric chair. Said, 'I no care!' (His English was as bad as his shooting.)
Adolf Hitler	German Nazi leader (1889–1945)	20 July 1944	*General von Stauffenberg* led senior German army officers in the attempt to blow Hitler up with a bomb planted in a suitcase. The bomb killed four people and blew off Hitler's trousers, but sadly horrible Hitler survived.
John Paul II	Pope (Born 1946)	13 May 1981	*Mehmet Ali Agca*. The Turkish gunman shot the Pope in St Peter's Square. Following the attack, the Pope travelled in a bullet-proof, glass-covered 'Pope-mobile'.
Margaret Thatcher	Prime Minister of UK (Born 1925)	12 October 1984	*Patrick Magee*. The IRA man planted a bomb in the Brighton hotel where the Conservative Party was staying for its annual conference. Five died in the blast, but the main target, Prime Minister Mrs Thatcher, survived.

Fidel Castro, President of Cuba since 1959

Castro has survived dozens of assassination attempts… Some say there have been more than 600. Many of them have been by his US enemies, the American CIA (the US Government's spies). It's said they have tried to assassinate him using:

- the Mafia (secret criminal gangs);
- an exploding cigar;
- an exploding seashell;
- a poisoned diver's wetsuit.

The CIA wanted his beard to drop out so he would look less tough. They made a powder to sprinkle in his shoes – it was never used.

Castro once said…

Castro has outlasted nine US presidents.

Eisenhower	Kennedy	Johnson	Nixon	Ford
1953–1961	1961–1963	1963–1969	1969–1974	1974–1977
Carter	Reagan	Bush Snr	Clinton	Bush
1977–1981	1981–1989	1989–1993	1993–2001	2001–

World assassin-target women's gold medal winner...

Queen Victoria, Queen of Great Britain and Ireland, 1837–1901
This 'popular' lady survived seven assassins – who had eight tries...

10 June 1840	29 May 1842
Edward Oxford	John Francis
Two loaded pistols – missed	Pistol – misfired
30 May 1842	3 July 1842
John Francis	John William Bean
Pistol – not loaded	Pistol – loaded with paper
19 May 1849	27 June 1850
William Hamilton	Robert Pate
Fired pistol – no bullet	Hit with brass head of walking stick
29 Feb 1872	2 March 1882
Arthur O'Connor	Roderick McLean
Pistol – not loaded	Revolver – missed

ASSASSINATION IS TERRIBLY COMMON

McLean had a poem written about him by the awful Scots poet William McGonagall... Maybe the cruellest punishment of all!

> McLean must be a madman,
> Which is obvious to be seen,
> Or else he wouldn't have tried to shoot
> Our most beloved Queen.

Two attempts (by John Francis) were made on two days running. Cruel Victoria wanted the useless killers executed 'as an example'. Most were sent to Australia … which is even more cruel. Not only did John Francis try to kill Queen Victoria (twice) but he was following in the footsteps of a soldier who tried to assassinate King George III, 40 years earlier. And that soldier's name was? Yes, John Francis.

John Francis the First was hanged, then had his head cut off.

Creepy? Two assassins with one name? That's NOTHING compared with…

— THE DEAD SPOOKY PRESIDENTS —

America has had two really popular presidents – Abraham Lincoln and John F Kennedy. Both were assassinated. But people have noticed some strange links between the killings – so many links, it is really rather creepy. Look at the facts and decide for yourself…

Abraham Lincoln	John F Kennedy
Abraham Lincoln was elected to Congress in 1846.	John F Kennedy was elected to Congress in 1946.
Abraham Lincoln was elected President in 1860.	John F Kennedy was elected President in 1960.

The names Lincoln and Kennedy each have seven letters.

Both were interested in fighting for civil rights.

Both of their wives lost a child while living in the White House.

| Abraham Lincoln | John F Kennedy |

Both Presidents were shot on a Friday.

Both Presidents were shot in the head.

| Lincoln's secretary was named Kennedy. | Kennedy's secretary was named Lincoln. |

Both were assassinated by men from a
southern state.

Both were followed by southern
vice-presidents named Johnson.

| Andrew Johnson, who followed Lincoln, was born in 1808. | Lyndon Johnson, who followed Kennedy, was born in 1908. |

| John Wilkes Booth, who assassinated Lincoln, was born in 1839. | Lee Harvey Oswald, who assassinated Kennedy, was born in 1939. |

Both assassins were known by their three
names.

Both names are made up of fifteen letters.

| Booth ran from the theatre where he had shot Lincoln and was caught in a warehouse. | Oswald ran from a warehouse and was caught in a theatre. |

Booth and Oswald were assassinated
before their trials.

So what do you reckon? Strange chance? Or history repeating itself?

Not a lot of assassins know…

John Wilkes Booth slept in a hotel before he went to assassinate President Lincoln. Wounded Lincoln was carried to the same hotel and placed on the SAME BED to die. Spooky!

FUNNY FASHIONS

When God made human beings she must have had a bit of a laugh. Ugly, pink creatures with no hair on their bodies. They walk on their back legs and have odd bits sticking out...

Let's be honest, we look a bit daft with no clothes on.

So what have humans done about it? They have taken these silly bodies and dressed them up! They no longer look a little silly – now they can look really, really stupid.

Humans have a word for 'making yourself look stupid' and the word is 'fashion'. Here are a few historical, hysterical howlers.

Pointy hats. In the Middle Ages, women in Europe wore 'steeple' hats that came to a point. A monk called Thomas Couette went around preaching that the 'steeple' hats were sinful because they were a sign of the deadly sin of pride. He told them to wear humble peasant caps instead. They obeyed and burned the steeples ... until Friar Thomas moved on somewhere else. Then the women went back to wearing the steeples – taller than ever!

Pointy toes. Another monk, Orderic Vitalis, had some very harsh words for Lord Fulk of Anjou. Lord Fulk's 'crime' was to invent shoes with long pointed toes that became a popular fashion. Spiteful Orderic said Fulk only wore them, 'to hide the shape of his twisted feet' (which were covered in lumps we call bunions). Pointed shoes came to have such long tips that young men had to chain the points to their knees to stop them tripping over them!

The Church said such shoes were sinful and called them 'devils' claws'.

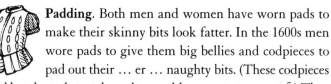 **Platform shoes**. Popular in all ages. Shoes raised up on platforms of cork were popular with ladies in Europe in the Middle Ages. Church leaders said they wasted cork and they wasted cloth – women needed more material to make the dresses reach the ground! Laws were passed to stop women wearing them.

Padding. Both men and women have worn pads to make their skinny bits look fatter. In the 1600s men wore pads to give them big bellies and codpieces to pad out their ... er ... naughty bits. (These codpieces had handy pockets, where they could carry a tasty orange[5].) They also wore leg pads to make them look hunky. In 1343 a monk (another one) moaned that women were sewing fox tails into their dresses to give them bigger bums. Some things never change...

 Corsets. For men and women who wanted to look thinner, there were corsets that squeezed their guts in and their chests out. In Italy Catherine de Medici (1519–1589) invented iron corsets, which kept the ladies of her court down to a 33-cm waist. Little girls were also strapped into them and some even died as a result.

Potted pee

Ever worn a Roman toga to a fancy dress party? Now you may look the part but will you SMELL the part?

You see, the Romans used human urine to wash their clothes, the way we use soap powder today.

5. Don't laugh. An orange in a codpiece was a tasty snack. Crisps hadn't been invented.

On the corners of streets in Roman cities there were large pots which men used to pee in as public toilets:

• The pee was collected and sold to the laundry workers.

• Boys were used to trample the clothes till they were clean.

• Of course, the pee was rinsed out. But it must have left a bit of a smell.

Try it. You are sure to win that fancy-dress contest because the other fancy-dressers will probably go home in disgust.

Body beautiful

Humans have put the most disgusting stuff on their faces and bodies to change the way they look.

Make-up. In ancient Babylon, in 2000 BC, people painted their faces with white lead to make them look pale. Italian women in the 1700s used arsenic (a deadly poison) to make their skins white – about 600 husbands and boyfriends died from kissing them! French women of the time used slimy, blood-sucking leeches on their faces to make them pale. Now pale people try to look brown by sitting in the sun and risk skin cancer.

Head lines. In the 1900s George Burchett would tattoo pictures on to the heads of bald men. (He should have drawn rabbits – from a distance they'd look like hares – hairs, geddit? Oh never mind.) Julius Caesar wore a crown of golden oak leaves to hide his bald head. Millions of other men (and women) wore wigs.

In AD 692 the Pope banned wigs – he said God's blessing couldn't get through the wig and into the head. Wig wearers were back in church by the 1700s but the wigs were so tall, they couldn't get in – the door of St Paul's Cathedral had to be raised 1.2 m.

 Hairy faces. Men have chopped and changed the hair on their face to try to stay in fashion. Deadly. John Steiner, a mayor in Austria in the Middle Ages, grew a moustache down to the ground. One day he tripped over it, fell down stairs and broke his neck. Most women want to get rid of face hair and in ancient times they did this by smearing cat poo on their faces. Fancy a kiss after that?

 Body mangling. In the 900s, in China, women had their feet bound up tightly in bangages to give them tiny feet. Why? Maybe to stop women running away from cruel husbands. When a girl was four years old, all her toes were broken, and her feet were bound tightly with cloth strips to keep her feet from growing larger than 10 cm. Clumsy binding could lead to toes rotting and dropping off. The feet smelled awful. Women were so crippled, they often needed help to walk. Yet this small-shoe shocker went on till it was finally banned in 1911, but by then millions of women had suffered it. Would you fancy that fancy footwork?

 Head crushers. In some ages people admired heads of a funny shape. They strapped boards to babies' skulls so they would grow up that way. The Incas of Peru and the Mangubetu of Africa gave their children pointed heads; in North America the Tilamook tribes of Oregon gave them flat heads, while the Chinooks gave them foreheads that sloped backwards. In the Dark Ages the Huns of Europe gave their children l-o-n-g heads.

Soften that skin

Want to have fine, soft skin? Then try this 1700 recipe for skin cream...

Puppidog water

Take a fat puppy dog of nine days old (or a baby pig that is nine days old).
Kill it and take the blood.
Break the legs and head, take out all the guts and liver, and throw them away.
Add four pints of Canary Wine[6], a pound of unwashed butter, two pints of snail shells and two lemons (with the skin cut off).
Boil these and let the steam drop into a glass bottle, in which let there be a lump of sugar, and a little gold leaf.
Rub into the skin.

Mysteries of the fashion world... *WHY IS IT CALLED LIPSTICK IF YOU CAN STILL MOVE YOUR LIPS?*

6. That's wine from the Canary Islands, of course, not wine made from smashed songbirds.

VICTORIAN SLANG

Some words pop into the language for a while, then disappear. There are a few historical words that we ought to remember. Suppose you are taken by time machine back to the 1800s. You wouldn't be able to speak to the villains in cities like London because they had their own words. (It confused the police, you see.) What you need is a Horrible Histories guide, and here it is:

area-sneak	thief who climbs down into basements to steal from kitchens
beak hunting	poultry stealing
bit fakers	makers of fake coins
black Maria	van that takes prisoners to gaol
bouncer	shoplifter
break a drum	commit burglary
bug hunters	people who roam around at night looking for drunkards to rob
bung nipper	pickpocket
button	fake coin
buttoner	person who gets a victim to play a game (eg cards) where they will be cheated
claws for breakfast	whipping while in prison
crack a case	commit burglary
cracksman	burglar
a dead lurk	breaking into a house while the family has gone to church
ding boy	mugger

dragsman	thief who robs cabs or carriages by climbing up behind, and cutting the straps that secure the luggage on the roof
fine wirers	long-fingered pickpockets
flying the blue pigeon	stealing lead from the roofs of houses
going snowing	going out to steal sheets drying in gardens
gospel grinder	missionary or scripture reader
gulpy	someone who will believe anything
hoisting	shoplifting
in for a vamp	in prison for theft
jolly	person who takes part in a fake street brawl so that a crowd will form which can be robbed
in lavender	hidden from the police
kidsman	person who trains young thieves
lagged	put in prison or transported
little snakesman	boy thief, paid by burglar to get in through small windows
lully priggers	thieves who steal clothes from washing lines
lurks	tricks of the trade
nibbed	arrested
to nose	to split on
to be on the blob	to beg by telling hard-luck stories
to be on the monkey	to beg
to be on the shallow	to go about half-naked so people feel sorry for you

pinch a bob	rob a till
queer screens	forged bank notes
the salt box	the condemned cell
shin scraper	prison treadmill
smasher	person who spends forged coins
starring the glaze	breaking a square of glass

 # DEADLY DUELS

Want to fight? Then let's do it properly. None of that kicking, biting, scratching and hitting with handbags (like modern footballers). Let's have a 'duel'...

Five famous duels (all involving British MPs):

Duke of Hamilton v Lord Mohun
15 November 1712 ✂ Hyde Park

Background: *An argument over who owned some land.*
What happened: *The men fought with short swords and both were killed. Lady Mohun complained about the mess her husband's bloody body made on her bedspread.*

Charles James Fox v William Adams
29 November 1779 ✗ Unknown

Background: *Charles James Fox called the Prime Minister (Lord North) 'useless' so Adams challenged him to a duel with pistols.*
Result: *Adams was told to stand sideways – less chance of being hit. Fatty Fox said: 'I am as thick one way as the other.' Fox was slightly injured.*

William Pitt (the Younger) v George Tierney
27 May 1798 ✗ Wimbledon Common

Background: *George Tierney disagrees with Prime Minister Pitt in the House of Commons. Eventually Tierney challenges Pitt to a duel with pistols.*
Result: *Both men missed.*

George Canning v Lord Castlereagh
21 September 1809 ✗ Putney Heath

Background: *Canning (Foreign Minister) and Castlereagh (War Minister) were both on the same side in the Duke of Portland's government. But they argued and Castlereagh challenged Canning to a duel with pistols.*
Result: *Both missed with their first shots, but Castlereagh wounded Canning in the thigh with his second. Both gave up their jobs in Parliament, but later returned. Canning went on to become Prime Minister in 1829.*

Duke of Wellington v 10th Earl of Winchilsea
29 March 1829 ✗ Battersea Fields

Background: *Winchilsea attacked Prime Minister Wellington for laws kind to Catholics, so the Duke challenged him to a duel with pistols.*
Result: *Both men fired into the air. (There are no reports of any dead sparrows.)*

—— POWER TO THE PETTICOAT ——

In 1792 Lady Almeria Braddock and Mrs Elphinstone had a pistol duel in London's Hyde Park. It became known as the 'petticoat duel'. Mrs Elphinstone was wounded.

But these warring women weren't the first – or the last – women to duel.

France 1700s

Mademoiselle Leriet was upset when her boyfriend went out with another woman. She challenged him to a duel. She let him shoot first. He was a real gentleman and he fired his pistol harmlessly into the air. Mademoiselle Leriet stepped up to him and shot him dead at point-blank range.

France 1700s (again)

Two Frenchwomen Baupret and Arli fought with short swords. Before the duel they had both been very beautiful, which seemed to be the reason for hating one another. During the duel they tried to strike only the face to mutilate one another. Both succeeded in that and lived to be ugly.

London 1833

Rosa Crosby was annoyed when another woman stole her husband so she challenged her to a sword duel. The other woman was good at fencing, while Rosa had never used a sword. But furious Rosa fought angrily and stabbed her rival to death.

USA 1817

Jane Wale and Cindy Dyer both wanted the same man and decided to fight for him. The winner would get him. The young man was there to watch. Cindy fell, badly wounded, and he was forced to marry Jane. (Maybe she'd have shot him if he refused!)

Austria 1800s

The president of 'The Vienna Musical and Theatrical Exhibition' was Princess Pauline Metternich. The president of the Women's Committee was Countess Kilmannsegg. They could not agree about how to organize the exhibition so they fought a duel. The Countess's arm was wounded and the Princess had her nose sliced.

 # FOUL FEASTING

Throughout history there have been some people who ate far more than anyone else. Far more than they needed to eat. Far more than an average person could eat. These sad people are known as gluttons.

In ancient history gluttony was 'good' – it showed the world how wealthy you were. Feasts were a way of showing off – the way rich people these days buy flashy cars. (BMWs hadn't been invented in ancient times.)

Kings like Henry VIII of England and Louis XIV of France were famous for their huge meals. But there were foul feasters more than a thousand years before those kings. Here are a few tasty samples...

1 Philoxenus of Cythera (Syracuse)

Philoxenus is supposed to have said, 'I wish I had a throat three cubits long [135 cm]' so the pleasure of swallowing his food could last longer.

Philoxenus is said to have used hot water to train his hands and throat to take scalding hot foods. That way he could go to a feast and eat everything before anyone else got a chance.

2 Caligula (Roman Emperor)

Said to have enjoyed drinking pearls dissolved in vinegar and to have served his guests with loaves and meats made out of gold.

To entertain his guests, Caligula had criminals beheaded in the dining room as they feasted. (And some people still like a nice chop for dinner.)

3 Claudius (Roman Emperor)

Hired slaves to tickle the tonsils of his guests with a feather. That way the guests would vomit, empty their stomachs and then carry on eating ... over and over again. The special room where this took place was called a vomitorium.

4 Vitellius (Roman Emperor)

Known as 'The Glutton'. Said to have enjoyed three or four banquets a day. At one, his brother served up 2,000 fish and 7,000 birds. Fave recipe: pike livers, pheasant brains, peacock brains, flamingo tongues and the spleen of eels.

His priests gave sacred cake to the gods. Vitellius couldn't resist pinching it for himself.

5 Nero (Roman Emperor)

Nero hired a 'glutton' – a huge Egyptian slave who ate everything he was fed. This was feast-time fun for Nero's guests. What Nero enjoyed most was watching his glutton kill a man and eat him.

6 Apicius (Roman cook)

Liked to pickle mullet fish alive at the table and watch them change colour.

Spent all his money on expensive foods and killed himself rather than eat like a peasant.

7 Elagabalus (Roman Emperor)

Said to have once served a meal comprising the brains of 600 thrushes. Ate camels' heels and cockerels' crests, flamingo brains, parrots' heads, peacocks' tongues and ostrich brains. He ate roast pig, from which live thrushes flew, and enjoyed African snails. Elagabalus rewarded his cooks for the invention of a new sauce … unless he didn't like it, in which case he forced them to eat nothing else but that sauce until they came up with one he did like.

8 Tiberius (Roman Emperor)

Said to have once feasted for two whole days and the night in between. When a poet called Tiberius 'fat', the Emperor had him thrown off a cliff to his death. His enemies said that Tiberius liked wine … but he liked blood even more.

9 Roman priests

Around 70 BC the priests were the biggest eaters in Rome. One of their tastiest treats was pig's udder. The priests also liked eating one food made to look like another. So the cooks made a 'fish' out of a pig's womb, a 'pigeon' out of bacon or a 'dove' out of ham.

The great feasting question... *IS IT TRUE THAT CANNIBALS DON'T EAT CLOWNS BECAUSE THEY TASTE FUNNY?*

Not a lot of cannibals know...

If a man of 68 kg (150 lb) is killed, then he could make a meal for around 75 people.

Foul feast fun

Tsar Peter I of Russia held a feast in 1697 to show everyone how he planned to punish the Streltzi, a group of people who had rebelled against him.

He held a three-day feast.

Day 1 1,500 men were beheaded in the dining room.

Day 2 700 rebels were strangled in the dining room.

Day 3 400 men had their ears and noses cut off in the dining room.

You don't have fun like that in restaurants today.

The great food question... *IF CORN OIL COMES FROM CRUSHING CORN, WHERE DOES BABY OIL COME FROM?*

DELIGHTFUL DINNERS AND TERRIBLE TEAS

If you were a poor person in the Middle Ages, you scraped by
with porridge and a few vegetables. If you were really lucky,
you got meat once or twice a week.

But the rich had all sorts of rare and unusual (and maybe
disgusting) foods.

Which would you like?

Porpoise pudding	stuffed porpoise stomach
Trojan hog	pig stuffed with birds and shellfish, then roasted
Deer-antler soup	singed antlers, chopped and boiled with wine
Cockentrice	back half of a pig sewn together with front half of a chicken and roasted
Coqz Heaumez	whole roast chicken dressed in helmet and lance, sitting astride a roasted hog
Mashed deer tongues	served on fried bread
Roast peacock	skinned then roasted, then put back in skin so it looks alive
Pickled puffin	a puffin cooked and soaked in vinegar
Curried head	a Saracen's head cooked in curry sauce (that's what Richard I of England ate in the Crusades)

Suffering squirrels

Zoologist Francis Buckland (1826–1880) loved trying new and interesting food. He ate...

squirrel pie, panther (that had been buried two days), **elephant trunk** (rubbery, he said), porpoise, **giraffe**, boa constrictor, **Japanese sea slug**, rhinoceros pie (like tough beef), **mole** (most disgusting, he reckoned), stewed bluebottles (nearly as disgusting), **fried earwigs** and mice on toast

Scrummy.

Not a lot of eaters know...

King Louis IV of France had a stomach that was twice as large as a normal stomach.

 SUFFERING SICKNESS

Sometimes Mr Death goes on a real spree and kills hundreds or thousands of people. Take London in 1665. People were dying of the terrible and mysterious plague – while the lucky ones were dying of some other good old-fashioned deaths.

How would you know if you had this deadly disease? You'd start spitting blood, or you'd see blood in your pee, or you'd start to swell up and get purple swellings in the armpit or the groin.

Which of these would you prefer?

Causes of death in 1655, in London

Plague 68,596

Worms 2,614		Bloody Flux 185
Spotted Feaver and Purples 1,929		Collick and Winde 134
Aged 1,545		Broken, bruised limbs 82
Griping in the Guts 1,288		Cold and Cough 68
Surfit 1,251		Vomiting 51
Stopping of the Stomack 332		Drowned 50
Rising of the Lights 397		Accidents 46

CRAZY CURES

Got an illness? You need a good old-fashioned crazy cure. Of course, it depends what age you live in. Here are a few top tips from the putrid past. Just don't try them at home or on your friends. Try them on someone who won't be missed – a teacher perhaps...

Cures for toothache

Stone Age Eat hollyhock flowers.
Saxon Boil holly leaf, lay it on saucer of water,
raise to mouth and yawn.
Stuart Scratch the gum with a new nail and then
drive the nail into a tree.
Georgian Burn ear with hot poker.

Cures for a headache

Stone Age and Roman Drill a hole in skull.
Saxon Find some swallow-chicks, cut their stomachs
open and look for some little stones. Tie the stones up
in a little bag and put it on your head.
Middle Ages Take off your hat so the harmful fumes
can escape from the head.
Inca Gouge hole between eyes with glass knife.
Tudor Lavender/bay/rue/roses/sage/marjoram.
Press a hangman's rope to the neck.

Cures for bites

Roman *Snakebite* Grind up fennel with wine and pour it
in the nostrils, while rubbing pig droppings on the wound.

THAT'S GROSS

Saxon *Snakebite* Get some wood from a tree grown in heaven and press it to the wound; *Spider bite* Let blood from a cut near the bite. Pour the blood into a hazelwood spoon and throw it over a road; *Dog bite* Burn the jaw of a pig and spread ashes on the wound.

Georgian *Snakebite* Kill a chicken, rip out its guts and place them on the wound while still warm.

Cures for diarrhoea

Ancient Egyptian Gruel, green onions, oil, honey, wax and water.

Inca Chew coca leaves.

Cures for ailments of the eyes

Ancient Egyptian *Poor eyesight at night* Crushed ox liver, roasted; *Cataracts* Tortoise brain and honey; *Blindness* Mash pig's eye with red ochre and pour into ear.

Saxon *Swollen eyelid* Cut it out with a knife.

Georgian *Stye* Rub with tail of black cat.

Cures for baldness

Saxon Burn bees and rub ash on head.

Tudor Smear head with fox grease, garlic and vinegar.

Cures for a fever

Inca *(for a baby)* Wash in bowl of family's pee and give it some to drink.

Stuart Cut a pigeon in half and place one half on each foot.

Cures for the plague

Middle Ages Wear a magpie's beak around the neck; burn sweet herbs; sit in a sewer; drink ten-year-old treacle; swallow emeralds crushed into a powder; eat arsenic powder; shave live chicken's bottom and strap it to plaguey sore; march from town to town flogging yourself with a whip.

Tudor Place freshly killed pigeon on the sores.

Cures for gout

Middle Ages Use a plaster with a mixture of goats' droppings, rosemary and honey.

Tudor Boil a red-haired dog in oil, add worms, pig's marrow and herbs. Place mixture on affected area.

Cures for a cold

Middle Ages Put mustard and onions up your nose.

Tudor *Bad chest* Thyme/campanula/hyssop.

Victorian Wrap a sweaty sock around the neck; *a sore throat* Wrap a red bandage round the neck.

I CAN'T SBELL THE SOCK, I HAVE ONIONS UB BY DOSE

Cures for bruises

Roman Treat with unwashed sheep's wool, dipped in the herb rue and animal fat.

Middle Ages Use a plaster, with bacon fat and flour.

Cure most likely to get you locked up

Ambrose Pare, of France, was called a 'great' surgeon because he learned how to treat soldiers wounded in battle. But one of his ointments for a wound was just a little sick:

 Ointment

YOU NEED:

Two new-born puppies, half a kilo of earthworms, one kilo of oil of lilies, half a kilo of turpentine, 25 grams of brandy.

TO MAKE:

Heat the oil and boil the puppies alive.

Add the worms, which have been drowned in white wine.

Boil and strain.

Add the brandy and turpentine.

Mix well.

Rub the mixture into the wound.

Make it and you will probably go to prison for cruelty to those poor worms.

DOCTOR! DOCTOR! WHO NEEDS YOU?

Doctors are busy people. Save their time by spotting your own disease. You may not feel better after reading these symptoms, but at least you'll know why you feel so bad…

If you have...   *please tick* ☐

High fever, chills, muscle pains, headache, painful red swellings in armpits and groin.

Then you could be suffering from...

BUBONIC PLAGUE *(or the Black Death) Widespread in Europe and Asia between 1347 and 1350. It killed up to a third of the population of Europe.*

....

If you have...   *please tick* ☐

Blue skin and diarrhoea that smells of fish.

Then you could be suffering from...

CHOLERA *Worst outbreaks in Europe were in the nineteenth century. Still occurs in parts of Africa and Asia where drinking water is dirty.*

....

If you have...   *please tick* ☐

Chill, fever, headache, sickness, vomiting, muscle aches, bloody poo, yellow skin, fits, coma.

Then you could be suffering from...

MALARIA *Still a huge health problem in hot countries. Around a million people die of malaria every year.*

....

If you have...   *please tick* ☐

Headache, high fever, cough, rash, chills, doziness, nightmares.

Then you could be suffering from...

TYPHUS *(or camp fever, ship fever, jail fever) At the Spanish siege of Granada in 1489, the Spanish army lost 3,000 men to the enemy and 17,000 to typhus.*

If you have... *please tick* ☐

High fever, tiredness, headache, backache, rash turning into pus-filled sores, vomiting, diarrhoea, bleeding.

Then you could be suffering from...

SMALLPOX *Wiped out in 1977. But some countries have kept the germs alive to use in germ warfare. Queen Elizabeth I suffered from it but recovered. Destroyed Inca Empire when Spanish invaders took it to Peru.*

....

If you have... *please tick* ☐

Sore throat, runny nose, cough, muscle pain, fever, bloodshot eyes, white spots in mouth, eyes sensitive to light, itchy, spotty rash.

Then you could be suffering from...

MEASLES *Not usually deadly these days. Taken to the US by settlers from Europe. From 1500 onwards, it killed thousands of Native Americans who were not used to the disease.*

....

If you have... *please tick* ☐

Fever, headache, runny nose, cough, chills, fatigue, sweating, loss of appetite, sore throat.

Then you could be suffering from...

INFLUENZA *(or flu) The First World War had killed 8.5 million when it ended in 1918. But Spanish Flu in 1918–1919 killed 30 million. Over 12 million died in India alone.*

....

normal   off colour   unwell   very poorly   critically ill   too late, mate

37°   38°   39°   40°   41°   42°

If you have... *please tick* ☐
Fever, rashes, muscle and joint aches, headache, sickness following a bite from a mosquito.

Then you could be suffering from...
DENGUE FEVER *(or breakbone fever or bonecrusher disease) First case recorded in 1779. Became more common in the twentieth century. Still no cure for this tropical disease.*

....

If you have... *please tick* ☐
Fever, headache, muscle aches, vomiting blood, red eyes, face and tongue, yellow skin, bleeding, fits, coma.
Then you could be suffering from...
YELLOW FEVER *Terrible disease in Africa, the Caribbean and the US in the nineteenth century. Slowed work on the Panama Canal when workers fell sick (the canal was completed in 1914).*

NICK THAT NECK

You wouldn't believe how horrible humans have been to each other through the ages. But some of the most brutal behaviour has been saved for punishing criminals – 'lopping the top' or beheading.

✠ The Roman Empire used beheading for its own citizens (with crucifixion[7] used for other ordinary people).

7. Crucifixion is being fastened to a cross and left to die – which would leave you very cross indeed.

In Britain, beheading was brought in by William the Conqueror but was only for those of noble birth who were guilty of treason.

91 people were beheaded in England between 1388 and 1747.

For neatness many victims had their head stitched back on before they were buried.

Beheading with an axe or sword was also used in Sweden, Denmark, Holland and France. Then, in 1792, France built beheading machines they called guillotines.

Germany continued to use beheading until the beginning of the Second World War. Two of the last beheadings in Germany were carried out on 18 February 1935, when the spies Baroness Benita von Falkenhayn and her friend Renate von Natzner were beheaded with an axe.

In Berlin, beheading with an axe was used up until 1938, when the guillotine and hanging became the only legal ways of execution in Germany.

China also used beheading widely, up until the communists came to power in the first half of the twentieth century and replaced it with shooting.

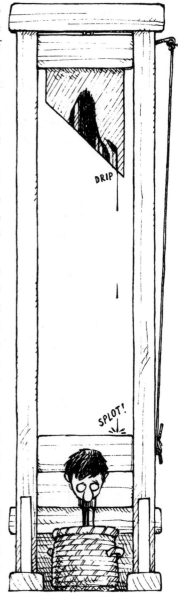

DRIP

SPLOT!

How they hacked – a guide

✂ There were three forms of beheading – by the **sword**, by the **axe** or by a **machine** (like a guillotine).

✂ Where an axe was used, a wooden block was made, often scooped out to fit the neck.

✂ Two patterns of block were used: the high block (about 450–600 mm, 18–24 inches high) where the prisoner knelt in front of it and leant forward so that their neck rested on the top; and the low block where the person lay full length and put their neck over the small wooden block just a few inches high.

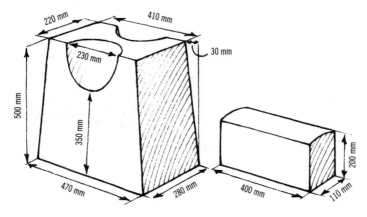

✂ The low block was used for the execution of Charles I in London, in 1649.

✂ All modern beheadings use the sword – for example, in Saudi Arabia, where 52 men and women were publicly beheaded in 2003.

✂ Where a person is to be topped with a sword, a block cannot be used. The victims are generally made to kneel down.

✂ But, if they are short, they could be executed standing.

✂ In Germany women were sometimes allowed to sit in a chair.

Anne Boleyn – the lopping of a lady

Twenty-nine-year-old Anne, Henry VIII's second wife, had been charged with treason and was sentenced to death by burning at the stake – or beheading if hubby Henry VIII was feeling kind…

Fortunately for Anne, Henry chose beheading and paid for an expert headsman from France. He would make the execution as quick and clean as possible. (English hangmen normally got the job of beheading but were poor at it because they didn't get a lot of practice.)

On 19 May 1536 Anne was led on to Tower Green at the Tower of London with an escort of 200 Yeoman of the Guard (Beefeaters). She wore a grey, fur-trimmed, robe over a red underskirt. Her hair was tied up and she wore a cross on a gold chain at her waist, and carried a white handkerchief and a prayer book.

She had to climb 150 cm (5 ft) up the steps to the scaffold to meet her headsman, who was wearing a black suit and half mask covering the upper part of his face. His long two-handed execution sword was hidden under the straw on the scaffold.

Anne made a short speech to the invited audience. She then removed her robe and put on a white cap. She knelt on the platform and prayed with her priest.

When she had finished, one of her ladies-in-waiting blindfolded her with a large handkerchief. The headsman took up the sword and beheaded her with a single blow.

Her ladies-in-waiting recovered her head – it is said that Anne's lips were still moving[8]. There was no coffin made for her so she was placed in an old arrow box and buried.

Visitors to the Tower can still see the position of the scaffold on Tower Green. Her ghost can also be seen there, if you fancy a chat.

8. Sadly we do not know what she was saying. Probably, 'Oi! Be careful, you're dripping blood all over that nice clean straw'.

CHOPPING LIST

Not everyone is lucky enough to lose their head with a single chop.
Sometimes bungling beheaders have bodged the butchery. Here are a handful of horrible hackings...

Victim	Crime	Executioner	Number of chops	Weapon used
Lord Balmerino	Fighting for Scotland against England, 1745	John Thrift – a very nervous man. He was so shaky, he needed wine to give him courage	3	axe
Rasmussen	Danish highwayman, 1887	The executioner was very drunk and made a mess of it. The crowd were so disgusted, Denmark never used beheading again.	3	axe
Henri Coiffier	French traitor, 1642	The executioner had never done it before and Coiffier nagged him to get on with it.	10	sword
Angelique Ticquet	French woman had old husband murdered, 1657	Sanson and son. Old Sanson couldn't kill the beautiful woman and left it to his son. As he was swinging she started chatting and he missed.	3	sword
Countess of Pole	Mother of an English traitor, 1541	Young assistant executioner – his boss, Cratwell, was on holiday. Old Countess was awkward and played 'catch me if you can'.	8+	axe

BRUTAL BYE-BYES

If you were just about to be executed, what would you say? 'Help!' or 'I didn't do it. I'm innocent'? Or would you just cry, 'Boohoo!'

One thing you probably wouldn't do is say something witty. But some criminals have.

Could you write your own headlines?

James French, died 1966
**'HOW ABOUT THIS FOR A HEADLINE FOR TOMORROW'S PAPER?
FRENCH FRIES.'**
Executed in electric chair in Oklahoma.

Jimmy Glass, died 12 June, 1987
'I'D RATHER BE FISHING.'
Executed in the electric chair in Louisiana.

Ned Kelly, Australian bushranger, died 1880
'SUCH IS LIFE.'
Executed by hanging in Melbourne.

Marie Antoinette, Queen of France, died 16 October, 1793
'SIR, I BEG YOUR PARDON.'
Spoken to the executioner, after she stepped on his foot on her way to the guillotine.

William Palmer, died 1856
'ARE YOU SURE IT'S SAFE?'
As he stepped on the trap door of the gallows just before he was hanged.

George Appel, died 1928

'WELL, GENTLEMEN, YOU ARE ABOUT TO SEE A BAKED APPEL.'

Executed in the electric chair in New York.

But the prize for the best joke goes to James Rodgers, an American who was about to be executed by a firing squad in 1960 in the USA.

'Have you any last request?' they asked him.

'Why yes,' he said.

'A BULLET-PROOF VEST.'

Boom-boom!

Not a lot of killers know...

The ancient Swedes used to 'help' old people to die by putting them in large pottery jars.

'Swede dreams, my wrinkly friend!'

TEACHER TORTURES

Old people (over 30) will tell you, 'When I went to school the teachers were tough...' And it's true that, until the 1970s, caning was common, the slipper was slapped and the ears were cracked. (Some sad children even had to eat school dinners.)

It was even worse in the 1800s when teachers did not believe in giving pupils a good talking to. One teacher said, 'A yard of strap is worth a mile of talk.'

Punishments included...

Kneeling

Kneel on rough floorboards with bare knees.
Place the hands on the back of the neck.
Keep the back straight.
Stay there for 20 to 30 minutes.
Get a slap on the head if you move.

The cane

Raise the hand you do NOT write with, palm upwards.
Teacher chooses a thin piece of bamboo cane.
Teacher brings down cane hard, maybe six times.
Notes: Boys must not cry out; the cane can also be used
on the bottom; sometimes a leather strap is used.

The punishment book

The 'crime' is written down with the date and the pupil's name in the punishment book.
When the pupil leaves school they will need a good report.
The pupil with a bad report will not get a good job and could go hungry and starve.

The log

A piece of wood weighing two or three kilos is tied across the shoulders of the pupil.
The pupil must sit and work with this till their feeble little shoulders ache.
This is a punishment for talking in class.

The cage

Attach a rope to the handles of a large basket.
Place the pupil in the basket and throw the rope over
a beam in the ceiling.
Haul the rope till the basket rises up to the ceiling.
Leave the pupil there for as long as it takes to make
them sorry.

The stocks

Place the child in stocks – two planks of wood that trap the ankles of the pupil.

Leave them there, cold, hungry (and probably wanting a pee).

Other pupils may laugh and poke fun at them.

The stocks were also used for criminals, of course. People would throw rotten fruit, dog droppings and mud at them. Joseph Lancaster was the man who told schools to use stocks – but said the victim should not have things thrown at them.

So that was all right then.

ROTTEN SCHOOL RULES

In the 1500s teachers used birches – more like whips – as punishment. One writer, Henry Peachum, remembered his 1500s schooldays and wrote...

'I know one teacher who, on a cold winter morning, would whip his boys just to keep himself warm. Another beat them for swearing and all the time he swore himself with terrible oaths.'

Schools have rules

In 1566 Oundle School ruled…

Scholars shall not go into ale houses or taverns and must not play unlawful games such as cards, dice or the like.

In 1528 Manchester Grammar School ruled…

For every oath or rude word that is spoken, in the school or elsewhere, the scholar shall have three strokes of the cane.

Toughest of all was Hawkshead School, which in 1585 ruled…

Punishment for making fun of another pupil – a beating. Punishment for losing your school cap – a beating.

One school in Tudor times tried to stamp out violence by writing…

No boy shall wear a dagger or any other weapon. They shall not bring to school any stick or bat, only their meat knife.

It seems that if you wanted school dinners, you had to take your own knife – a pretty sharp one to cope with the tough old sheep they fed you in Tudor schools.

Dire dinners

School dinners have always been the subject of fun for pupils. In the 1950s insulting names for school dinners were collected. Sago pudding was a great favourite and named:

frogspawn OR **fishes' eyes in glue** OR **snottie gog pie**.

Charming.

A terrible top ten of 1950s filth may be…

SOS	'Same Old Slosh'
YMCA	'Yesterday's Muck Cooked Again'
ARMOURED COW	tinned beef
BILGE	gravy
FRIZZLED MONKEY	fried bread
SPLIDGE	cheese pie
STRING/WORMS	spaghetti
OLD MAN'S POO	sponge pudding
FLIES' CEMETERY	currant cake
GREEN SLING	custard

SHE'S PUT WORMS IN MY POO

But the winner is probably jam roly-poly, lovingly known as 'dead baby'.

Sing-a-song of sickness

Some pupils have even chanted rhymes about the nice nosh that's sploshed in front of them. In Victorian times they sang…

Slishy splashy custard, dead dogs' eyes,
All mixed up with giblet pies.
Spread it on the butty nice and thick,
Swallow it down with a bucket of sick.

REVOLTING RHYMES

It isn't just maths and history and science that children have learned at schools through the ages. They have also learned some disgusting stuff outside the classrooms. Vile verse and putrid poems...

As I sat under the apple tree,
A birdie sent his love to me,
And as I wiped it from my eye,
I said, 'Thank goodness cows can't fly.'

Oh the black cat piddled in the white cat's eye,
The black cat said, 'Gord blimey.
I'm sorry, sir, I piddled in your eye,
I didn't know you was behind me'.

Ladies and gentleman,
Take my advice.
Pull down your pants
And slide on the ice.

The higher up the mountain,
The greener grows the grass,
The higher up the monkey climbs,
The more he shows his ***.
Ask no questions,
Hear no lies,
Shut your mouth,
And you'll catch no flies.

Mary had a little lamb,
Its feet were black as soot.
And into Mary's bread and jam
Its sooty foot it put.
Mary had a little lamb,
Her father shot it dead.
And now it goes to school with her
Between two chunks of bread.
Mary had a little lamb,
She also had a bear.
I've often seen her little lamb,
But I've never seen her bear.

Rhymes of the times

Pupils were always good at putting the latest events into their rhymes that they chanted as they skipped or bounced a ball. So, for example, in 1873 a woman called Mary Ann Cotton was hanged for murdering three husbands and about a dozen or more of her children (the exact number of her victims isn't known). The playground verse of the time was...

Mary Ann Cotton, she's dead and she's rotten.
She lies on her bed with her eyes wide open.
Sing, sing, what shall I sing?
Mary Ann Cotton is tied up with string.
Where? Where? Up in the air,
Selling black puddings a penny a pair.

The arms and legs of a hanged person would swell up and turn dark – like black pudding. Nasty.

During the First World War (1914–1918) rhymes were made up against the German leader Kaiser William (or Bill)...

Kaiser Bill went up the hill
To conquer all the nations;
Kaiser Bill came down the hill
And split his combinations[9].

Then, in the Second World War (1939–1945), they made fun of German leader Adolf Hitler – who wasn't very funny at all...

Who's that knocking at the window?
Who's that knocking at the door?
If it's Hitler, let him in
And we'll sit him on a pin,
And we won't see Hitler any more.

Knock-out games

Knocking on the door and running away was an exciting game for children – probably since doors were invented. But it's a bit of a mouthful to say, 'Do you want to play knocking-on-the-door-and-running-away-before-anyone-catches-you?'

9. Combinations are long-legged underpants. Nice and warm in winter – hot and smelly in summer. Well, you did ask.

So throughout history children have invented weird names for this fun game…

Nick-Nock-Nanny ✸ **Chickydoory** ✸ Ring-Bell-Scoot
Knock-Down-Ginger ✸ Tap-Door-Run ✸ **Jinks Tat**
Bobby Knocker ✸ **Bing-Bang-Skoosh**
Nicky-Nocky-Nine-Doors ✸ **Tappit-and-Skedaddle**

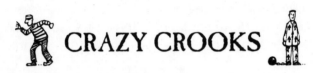

CRAZY CROOKS

There are lots of peculiar people in the world. They just have to go around breaking the laws. Still, life is never boring when these crazy criminals are around. People like...

 Reverend Edward Free (1755–1843). This priest from Bedfordshire made money by selling the lead from his church roof and the trees from the churchyard. He kept sheep in the church porch, and cows and pigs roamed around the graves – even during a funeral. Reverend Free whipped his helpers and ended up in a gun siege in the church. He finally fled to London, where the wheel came off a coach and killed him. Free-wheeled, you might say.

Samuel Solomon (1781–1853). Sam invented 'The Balm of Gilead' which, he said, was an ancient cure from 1730 BC. It cured everything from yellow fever to 'horrors of the mind' and was also a love potion. Solomon sold thousands of bottles and made a fortune.

People loved it – but became balm addicts. The 'balm' turned out to be brandy. The people who bought it? Balmy?

 Jane Wenham (1642–1730). Her crime was to turn herself into a talking cat and tell Ann Thorn (aged 16) to kill herself. At least that's what Ann said, and the court believed her. Jane was sentenced to death as a witch but a gentle judge let her off. Ann later said she only accused Jane because she was in a bad mood – her boyfriend had upset her. No one was ever sentenced to death for witchcraft again in England. Witch just goes to prove ... something.

Lancelot Blackburne (1658–1743). was a priest in the Caribbean, but found the pay was poor. So he joined a pirate ship and attacked Spanish galleons. He returned to England to work as a priest. Was he hanged for piracy? No, he was made Archbishop of York. God knows why.

 George Psalnanazar (1680–1763). He made lots of money writing books and giving talks about his 'home' country, Formosa. His tales were exciting – 'People who attacked the king would be hanged by the feet till they died and had four dogs to tear them to pieces,' he said. For his talks he wrapped a snake round his neck 'the way Formosans do, to keep cool'. But George had never been to Formosa – no one from Britain ever had – and in time he was found out. Still, it had been fun while it lasted.

Captain Richard Dudley (1681–1708). At the age of nine he robbed his sister and ran away with her money. (Keep it in the family.) He joined his brother in highway robbery and they were hanged together. At their funeral their father fell on to their coffins in the grave, died and was buried with them. That's REALLY keeping it in the family.

 Shanghai Kelly (born 1835). This Irishman made a good living by finding men to work on ships – even though they didn't want to. He would drug them with beer and sell them to ships' captains. The poor men woke up at sea. Captains paid $100 for each man. From time to time Kelly would slip in the odd dead body. He also put in a dummy with a rat up the sleeve – the twitching rat made the dummy look alive and the captains paid up.

Lady Margaret Lambourne (born 1550). Elizabeth I had Mary Queen of Scots executed in 1587. Lady L decided to kill Elizabeth in revenge. She dressed as a man and carried two pistols into the palace – one shot for the Queen, one for herself. One pistol went off early and killed a peacock. Elizabeth I forgave Lady L – the peacock probably didn't. She was seized as soon as the first pistol went off. Lady L said she was doing her duty. Queen E asked, 'What is my duty?' Lady L replied, 'To pardon me.' The Queen admired her dedication and pardoned her.

 Anne Robinson (born 1750). Anne was a serving girl, living in her sister's home. When pots and pans, plates and lumps of food started flying around the house, Anne said the house was haunted. She was hoping her sister would move out to make room for Anne's boyfriend. But Anne was thrown out and the 'ghost' vanished. Anne later owned up to faking the ghost.

James Alexander (born 1700). This cruel criminal was taken to court by a labourer who complained that James had piddled in his hat. The court let James off when he agreed to buy the victim a new (dry) hat.

DIRE DISASTERS I

Here are a few of the deadliest disasters in human history. Use this as a helpful guide: where not to go for your next holiday!

Five worst volcanic eruptions
Don't go here unless you enjoy smoking...

Date	Volcano	Place	Deaths
79 (24 August)	Mount Vesuvius	Italy	20,000
1669 (25 March)	Mount Etna	Sicily	20,000
1883 (26 August)	Krakatoa	Indonesia	36,000
1902 (8 May)	Mount Pelée	Martinique, West Indies	30,000+
1985 (13 November)	Nevada del Ruiz	Colombia	23,000

Five worst earthquakes

Don't go here unless you like your drinks shaken but not stirred…

Date	Place	Richter scale	Deaths
526	Antioch, Turkey	Unknown	830,000
1556	Shensi, China	Unknown	300,000
1737	Calcutta, India	Unknown	242,000
1927	Nan-Shan, China	8.3	200,000
1976	Tangshan, China	8.2	250,000

Five worst tsunamis (tidal waves)

Don't go here unless you own a very big surfboard…

Date	Place	Height of wave	Deaths
1707	Japan	11.5 m	60,000
1775	West Europe/Morocco/ West Indies	16 m	Unknown 36,000
1783	Italy	unknown	30,000
1883[9]	Indonesia	35 m	36,000
1896	Japan	30 m	27,000

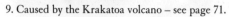

9. Caused by the Krakatoa volcano – see page 71.

Five worst hurricanes

Perfect for people who enjoy fresh air...

Date	Place	Deaths
1737 (7 October)	Bengal, India	300,000+
1881	Haiphong, Vietnam	300,000
1882 (6 June)	Bombay, India	100,000+
1876	Bengal, India	200,000
1970 (13 November)	Bangladesh	500,000–1 million

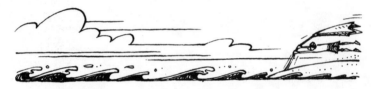

Five worst floods

Of course, this list does not include Noah's flood...

Date	Place	Deaths
1099	England and The Netherlands	100,000
1287 (14 December)	The Netherlands	50,000
1642	Kaifeng, China	300,000+
1887 (September – October)	Hwang Ho River, China	900,000+
1939	North China	500,000

Five worst avalanches

Don't forget your skis if you go to…

Date	Place	Deaths
1618 (4 September)	Plurs, Switzerland	1,500
1916 (13 December)	Italian-Austrian Alps	10,000
1950–1951(several)	Swiss-Austrian Alps	250+
1962 (10 January)	Ranrahirca, Peru	2,700
1970 (31 May)	Yungay, Peru	20,000

Think yourself lucky. Nature wiped out the dinosaurs completely!

MAD MONARCHS

Madness is sad. In the past, people with mental illness have often been treated with incredible cruelty – and have often been treated well too.

But there have been so many mad rulers, you have to wonder – do you have to be mad to rule? Or does ruling make you mad?

Here are just a few of the ones who were mad, sad … and sometimes rather bad.

Caligula, Roman Emperor (ruled AD 37–41)

- Thought he was god.
- His girlfriend was his sister.
- Had people executed for fun.
- Made his horse a consul.[11]

Nero, Roman Emperor (r. AD 54–68)

- Murdered his half brother.
- Tried to drown his mother at sea, sent soldiers to stab her to death instead.
- Murdered his wife when he got a girlfriend, then kicked his girlfriend to death.
- Dressed up as a lion and attacked people at gladiatorial fights.

Charles VI, King of France (r. 1380–1422)
- Killed four of his own men with his sword.
- Imagined he was made of glass and would shatter if anyone touched him.
- Sometimes howled like a wolf.
- Known as Charles the Mad.

Joanna, Queen of Castile (r. 1505–1555)
- Went everywhere with the mummy corpse of her husband.
- Wouldn't let any women near it, in case they flirted with him.
- Known as Joanna the Mad.

George III, King of England (r. 1760–1820)

- Sometimes ended every sentence with word 'peacock'.
- Believed London was flooded and ordered a yacht.
- Wore a pillowcase around his head and tried to adopt a pillow as a son.
- Believed he had actually died and wore black mourning clothes out of respect.

11. Or did he? This is a popular story about Caligula. But the Horrible Histories truth is Caligula SAID he could make his horse Incitatus a consul (Roman official) but never did. It was probably his idea of a joke.

Ibrahim I, Sultan of Turkey (r. 1640–1648)
- Mentally ill, he was kept in a cage for 23 years, then was released to become Sultan.
- Stabbed his own son in the face … for telling a bad joke!
- Heard one of his 280 wives had a boyfriend. He didn't know which, so he had all the 280 wives tied in sacks and drowned (one escaped).
- Was thrown off his throne, put back in the cage and strangled with a bow string.

Ivan IV (Ivan the Terrible), Tsar of Russia (r. 1547–1584)
- Married eight times and killed wives when he grew tired of them.
- Got angry with his son and killed him.
- Murdered thousands of his subjects.

Christian VII, King of Denmark (r. 1766–1808)
- Liked to go on robbing sprees in Copenhagen, the capital of his kingdom.
- While king, he threw a bowl of sugar over his granny and stuck pins in her chair.
- Liked to play leapfrog over visitors who bowed before him.
- Slapped his ministers and diplomats when discussing affairs of state.
- Staged mock executions of his own courtiers.
- Servants were trained NOT to obey his orders.
- Stood in window of palace making faces.
- Banged his head against the wall till it bled.

Norton I, Emperor of the USA (r. 1859–1880)
- Proclaimed himself Emperor of the USA (though it's a republic and he lived in a boarding house in San Francisco).
- Totally penniless, but issued his own personal banknotes.
- Issued various decrees dissolving the Republic and abolishing Congress, as well as the Democrat and Republican parties.
- Banned the word 'Frisco'.

OTHER ODD LEADERS

✵ **Catherine the Great (1729–1796)** married Grand Duke Peter of Russia. He taught her how to use weapons, then made her guard their bedroom door all night long. He also hung a rat from their bedroom ceiling – Peter said the rat was guilty of stealing some food and would stay hanging there for three days. Sweet dreams, Cath. She died on the toilet. Rats!

✵ **Peter the Great of Russia (1672–1725)** was terrified of being assassinated – even when he visited London. He was invited to go to the British Parliament, but didn't want to be trapped in a building full of people. Instead he was hoisted on to the gutter of a house opposite and looked in through the windows at Parliament. Even the British king laughed at him. Peter returned home with British ideas. For a start, he banned beards because his Brit friends usually shaved them off. If he saw one of his nobles with a beard, he would try to tear it out with his bare hands.

✵ **Emperor Ferdinand of Habsburg (1793–1875)** never grew up. His favourite game was climbing into a large waste-paper basket and rolling around the floor. He also liked catching flies in his hands. His Prime Minister (who really ran the country) called Ferdy 'a lump of putty'. But the Emperor said some really clever things like, "I am Emperor, I want noodles, so I get them." One of Ferdinand's sisters, Marianna (1804–1858), was so scary-looking, she was kept locked in a room.

✵ **Empress Elizabeth of Austria (1837–1898)** had a thing about her hair. She had it washed in 20 bottles of fine brandy and raw egg yolks. Her hairdresser then brushed it and Elizabeth had the fallen hairs counted. If she lost too many hairs, she became very upset. Liz also took lessons in being a circus stunt rider. She became very good and gave shows – for her pet dogs.

Emperor Menelik II of Ethiopia (1844–1913) had a curious cure. If he ever felt ill, he ate a few pages from the Bible. He died after a stroke while he was being fed pages from the Old Testament. What chapters was he eating? 'The Book of Kings' of course.

King Ludwig II of Bavaria (1845–1886) liked the idea of going on long journeys and stopping off for a picnic. But he never went anywhere – except round and round his stables in circles for hours and hours. He would stop to change horses, have his picnic, then ride on.

Tsar Paul I of Russia (1754–1801) banished some of his soldiers to the frozen region of Siberia. What was the 'crime' of these suffering soldiers? They marched out of step. Poor Paul was murdered ... just like his dad (Peter III) ... so that saved a lot of frozen soldier toes.

DEAD AS A DODO

Human beings have been around for a couple of million years and may be around for another couple of million if they don't wipe themselves out. But some creatures have not been so lucky. Some creatures are 'extinct' – gone for ever.

That's why we say, 'Dead as a dodo.' (What do you mean, YOU don't say dead as a dodo? Just take my word for it – MOST people say dead as a dodo when something is completely finished, snabbled and kaput.)

For some reason we never say, 'Dead as a big-eared hopping-mouse,' or, 'Dead as a white-footed rabbit-rat', even though those two Australian creatures are just as dead. Funny that...

Anyway, here are just ten of the thousands of creatures that are dead as yellowfin cut-throat trout (last seen in Colorado, 1910)...

BROAD-FACED POTOROO *Last seen: 1865, south-west Western Australia.* When convicts arrived from Europe they set about clearing the lands where the potoroo pottered about. With a name like that, it never had a chance.

HARPAGORNIS *Last seen: around 1600, New Zealand.* This monster was the largest bird of prey ever known. It weighed 10 to 14 kg (31 lb) and attacked at speeds of up to 80 kmph (50 mph). The harpagornis lived in New Zealand and hunted moas. The Maoris killed off the harpagornis because it was a very dangerous monster to have in your skies. It was nicknamed the leopard eagle – it isn't spotted now.

MOA *Last seen: around 1600, New Zealand.* It was a grass-eater and pretty harmless (unless it sat on your bald head in mistake for an egg). It was just a big fat dinner on legs. It couldn't fly so the Maoris (who arrived around AD 1000) killed off the moa for food. No more moa.

GREAT AUK *Last seen: 1844, Eldey Island.* The last pair were killed on 3 July, 1844 by collectors. This bird was hunted to extinction for food and because its feathers made lovely fluffy mattresses. Alive yesterday, dead today, bed tomorrow.

TASMANIAN TIGER *Last seen: 1933, Tasmania.* It wasn't even a tiger! But once dingos arrived in Australia, the TT was driven out. It lived on in dingo-free Tasmania, but farmers killed it (to keep it from killing their cattle), hunters killed it (for a reward) and collectors collected it for zoos (because they thought they were 'saving' it – they weren't). Some people still say they see it today in Tasmania – and in Britain. (If that's true then someone should tell the TT it is very, very lost.)

QUAGGA *Last seen: 1883, Amsterdam Holland.* The last one died on 12 August 1883 at the Artis Magistra Zoo. Its home was in South Africa. It looked like a zebra at the front and a horse at the back. Farmers killed it so it wouldn't eat their cattle's grass – and it made nice handbags too. Quagga just quit.

LESSER STICK-NEST RAT *Last seen: 1933, Australia.* Once rabbits arrived in Australia they ate all the rat's grass. In 1859, 24 rabbits were set loose in Australia. Six years later there were two million. The lesser stick-nest rat just couldn't stick around after that.

CAROLINA PARAKEET *Last seen: 1918, USA.* The last one died in the Cincinnati Zoo. The trouble was it was just too pretty. The only parrot living in eastern USA, this parakeet was hunted to extinction for its feathers. (It also liked to nibble the farmers' crops.)

PASSENGER PIGEON *Last seen: 1914, USA.* The most amazing extinction of all because it was once the most common bird in the world. There were maybe five BILLION passenger pigeons in the USA. They lived in huge flocks of up to two billion birds. Such a flock would be a mile wide and 300 miles long, taking several days to pass. But the pigeon was hunted for food and numbers started to fall. Almost all of the remaining quarter-million passenger pigeons were killed in a single day in 1896 by sport hunters, who knew they were shooting the last wild flock. The last passenger pigeon, named Martha, died in the Cincinnati Zoo. Her stuffed body is on display at the Smithsonian Institution museum. As dead as a dodo...

DODO *Last seen: 1681, Mauritius.* Once the Dutch settlers arrived, their rats and cats raided dodo nests. But the dodo was so friendly it stood still and let the Dutch smash its head and eat it, becoming extinct less than 80 years after the humans arrived. The dodo would not have won any beauty contests but it didn't deserve to dodo die. Now as dead as ... a big-eared hopping-mouse.

GROTTY GRAFFITI

Graffiti looks pretty messy but it isn't a modern problem. There has been graffiti ever since humans could write ... sort of 'Ug was here, one million years BC.'

The Romans had graffiti. How do we know? Because in AD 79 the Roman town of Pompeii was smothered in ash when the volcano Vesuvius erupted. Hundreds of years later the ruins were dug up and the graffiti was uncovered. Here are the sort of things those Romans wanted you to know...

C PUMIDUS DIPILUS HEIC
FUIT A D V NONAS OCTOBREIS
M LEPID Q CATUL COS

Gaius Pumidius Dipilus was here,
3 December 78 BC.

EPAPHRODITUS
CUM THALIA HAC

Epaphroditus was here
with Thalia.

AUGII AMAT ALLOTENUM
Auge loves Allotenus.

VIRGULA TERTIO SUO
INDECENS ES

Virgula to her
boyfriend Tertius:
You're disgusting!

SAMIUS
CORNELIOS
SUSPENDRE

Samius to Cornelius:
Go hang yourself!

CHIE OPTO TIBI UT REFRIGENT SE FICUS TUAE

Chie, I hope your piles rub themselves raw.

MIXIMUS IN LECTO.
SI DICES: QUARE? NULLA
FUIT MATELLA

We have peed in our beds... If you ask: why? There was no potty.

CACATOR CAVE MALUM, AUT SI
CONTEMPSERIS, HABEAS IOVEM
IRATUM

Watch it, you that dumps in this place! May you have Jove's anger if you ignore this.

SUSPIRIUM PUELLARUM CELADUS THRAEX

Celadus the Thracian gladiator makes the girls sigh!

PITUITA ME TENET

I've caught a cold.

ADMIROR
PARIES TE NON
CECIDISSE RUINIS QUI TOT
SCRIPTORUM TAEDIAE
SUSTINEAS

I am amazed, wall, that you have not fallen in ruins.

WARRING WOMEN

Someone once said, 'If women were in charge, there would be no wars.' To be honest, it was a woman who said it. To be even more honest, she was w-r-o-n-g.

On the walls of Hittite palaces in around 1300 BC there are paintings of woman warriors carrying axes and swords[12]. They weren't the first and they weren't the last.

If any clever person tells you women don't fight wars, then give them a few cool but cruel cases from horrible history...

The Rig Veda is an ancient sacred poem of India, written between 3500 and 1800 BC. It tells the story of warrior-queen Vishpla, who lost her leg in battle, was fitted with an iron leg and returned to battle. Iron lady.

The Hebrew wise-woman, Deborah, was a war leader during the occupation of Canaan, 1250–1050 BC. With her advice the Hebrews smashed the armies of Canaan. Bet no one dared to call her Debbie.

The Greeks had legends of a group of women warriors called the Amazons. Some historians think these legends were based on Scythian women of the fourth and fifth centuries BC. Archaeologists have found female skeletons with bows, swords, and horses.

12. The Hittites hung about the Middle East from around 3000 to 1000 BC smashing a lot of other people, including the Babylonians who thought that being hit by a Hittite was hideous.

In AD 39 **Trung Trac and Trung Nhi** led a  Vietnamese revolt against the Chinese. They captured 65 forts and reigned as queens until AD 43. Their mother Tran Thi Doan (also known as Lady Man Thien) trained them in military skills and led troops to support them. Phung Thi Chinh also took part in the Vietnam battles of AD 43 and had her baby at the battlefront. The mother of all battlers.

In AD 366 **Empress Jingo Kogo** led a  Japanese invasion of Korea. She was pregnant at the time and therefore had to have adjustable armour made.

In AD 63 **Celtic and Roman gladiator shows** included 'women of high class'. There was also a female chariot fighter rider who fought against men. In AD 88 women gladiators were described as members of the venatores (gladiators who fought wild animals in the Roman arena). Emperor Alexander Severus passed a law banning women fighters in the arena in AD 200.

Legendary Celtic women warriors included Medb (Maeve) of Ireland, Aife (Aoife) of Alba (Scotland), and Queen Scathach of Skye. The Romans in Britain fought against Queen Boudica (or Bodiecia, Boadicea, Voadica, Voada) of the Iceni in AD 61. The Romans were allies to Queen Cartimandua of the Brigantes in a war against her boyfriend in AD 43.

In the 900s Queen Thyre of Denmark led her army against the Germans, and in 722 Queen Aethelburgh destroyed Taunton. Also in the 900s Aethelflaed, Lady of Mercia, led troops against the Vikings and Olga of Russia ended a revolt in which her husband had died.

In the 1500s Graine Ni Maille (also known as Grace O'Malley) was an Irish pirate, while Marguerite Delaye and Captain Mary Ambree fought in sea battles. Beatriz de Pardes and María de Estrada fought with the Conquistadors in the New World while the men exploring in South America reported seeing native women leading war bands.

In 1297 the Scottish Countess of Ross led her own troops during William Wallace's (Braveheart's) battles with the English. Lady Bruce defended Kildrummy Castle from the English during the Wars of Independence. During the same war, the widow of David of Strathbogie defended the island fortress of Lochindorb against 3,000 Scots. Lady Agnes Randolph, known as Black Agnes, held her castle at Dunbar against the forces of England's Earl of Salisbury for over five months. Philippa of Hainault, Queen of Edward III, led 12,000 soldiers against invading Scots in 1346 and captured their King, David Bruce. Who needed men in kilts when the women in kilts were so good?

EVIL EXECUTIONS

There's more than one way to skin a cat, they say. And there's more than one way to kill a criminal. You may think you know them all – but there are a few unusual ones you may not know about.

The use of women to carry out executions is very rare. But in the nineteenth century, the Watusi tribe of Africa used women to carry out a killing that brought terrible shame to the victims...

Weighty Watusi women

For hundreds of years the Watusi had been bitter enemies with the Pygmies as they battled over the same lands. By strange chance, the Watusi are the tallest people on earth, with many of the men standing over 2.13 m (7ft), while the Pygmies are the shortest people on earth, with full-grown men often less than 1.22 m (4ft) in height.

When a Pygmy warrior was captured, the prisoner would be stripped of all his weapons and clothing, bound with ropes, and then thrown into a large, stone-floored pit. Waiting in the pit were Watusi women.

The very tall women would then trample on the small man, crushing him to death beneath their feet. This was thought to be a very shameful way to die, owing to the fact that the warrior was losing his life at the hands of women[13] ... and of course because he was being squashed like an insect not a man.

Many Pygmies who showed no fear in battle dreaded the thought of such a death.

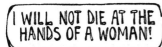

I WILL NOT DIE AT THE HANDS OF A WOMAN!

OR THE FEET

Squidging sultan

In northern India there was a savage sultan called Ghiyas-ud-Din of Malwa (1469–1500).

The Sultan had two large wooden platforms built (about 6 m by 6 m).

One was placed above the other in two layers (like a jam sponge cake). The top layer could slide up and down over the bottom one by way of rails at each corner.

The victim (who had upset the Sultan) would be laid on his

13. Yes, all right, he was losing his life at the feet of women, not their hands. At their hands is just a figure of speech. Don't worry about it.

back, on top of the lower platform, right in the middle. Then the upper platform was lowered on its rails, until it came down on to him.

❧ The weight of the upper platform was not quite enough to crush the prisoner (it must have been about 270 kg) but was heavy enough to pin him firmly in place.

❧ At this point, the Sultan would have women from his palace enter. Then, one by one, each woman would step up on to the upper platform and there take her place.

❧ An opening was cut in the upper platform for the victim's head, so that he would not die too quickly from a crushed skull … and also so that he would have to watch helplessly as the women gathered around him and their weight on his body grew heavier and heavier.

❧ Although the Sultan's palace was home to 6,000 beautiful women, only about 150 women could have squeezed their way on to a platform that size at one time. This is probably why the Sultan chose the tallest among his women as executioners – so as to provide the most weight. One hundred and fifty tall women would weigh nearly 11 tonnes.

The prisoner would end up like jam in that sponge cake – and probably the same colour.

Trunk-ated and terminated

What would you do if you didn't have 6,000 beautiful women to crush your criminals? Bring in an elephant, of course.

Elephants were used for 4,000 years in Asia. The ancient Romans even borrowed the idea from time to time.

For many centuries elephants were also used by armies, and death by elephant was used for deserters or prisoners-of-war.

The British ruled India from the 1800s and carried on with elephant executions to keep the local people happy.

✖ The last person to be officially executed in this fashion was put to death in India, in April 1947.

✖ The execution took place in Bikaner.

✖ The executioner was a state elephant named Hawai that weighed just over 8 tonnes.

✖ Under British rule, it had put more than 150 thieves and murderers to death beneath the crush of its huge foot.

✖ The execution elephant was trained to place its enormous foot gently upon the prisoner's head.

THAT TICKLES!

✖ At this point, those who had accused the victim would be brought forward and allowed to look beneath the elephant's foot to agree this was the right man.

✖ They could then either give the go-ahead or spare him. (Often the victim would scream and beg for mercy, but that hardly ever happened. If a witness said, 'He's innocent,' then the witness would take his place under the elephant's foot for lying in the first place!)

✖ Once the witnesses said, 'Yes,' the mahout (elephant driver) would give the command. The elephant would press down with its immense weight, bursting the skull and then crushing the head completely flat.

🐘 However, from time to time, the death would be made even more cruel by having the elephant drag the victim through the streets with a rope attached to the elephant's leg.

🐘 Or, just as bad, the elephant was trained to crush limbs first, and then the chest, often very slowly.

🐘 There are records of children being executed in this way.

Jumbo jury

One Mogul Emperor, Akbar (1542–1605), used his favourite elephant as a judge, as well as an executioner. While ruling in the city of Agra from 1570 to 1585, Akbar believed the elephant could spot a guilty person. As a result, people were staked out before the great royal elephant and had to watch in horror as it was led to step on them. Thousands died in this way.

Most were crushed to death, but from time to time the huge elephant would refuse. They were released – the elephant had decided they were 'not guilty'.

 # IDIOTIC INVENTIONS

Humans are supposed to be the cleverest people on the planet. So how come they have so many idiotic ideas? Some inventions will never work. We know this because clever people have told us they will never work. Things like...

Flying machines

In 1895 Lord Kelvin (1824–1907) a top British scientist, said,

'Heavier-than-air flying machines are impossible.'

And Lord Kelvin made sense. But that hasn't stopped potty people dying to fly … and flying to die.

In 1896 (a year after Kelvin said it was impossible) Otto Lilienthal of Pomerania crashed his glider, broke his back, and died. Lord Kelvin probably said, 'I told you so.'

Otto had attempted about 2,000 flights by then. He started at the age of 13 by making wings and flapping his arms very hard. He then built machines like today's hang-gliders and bounced up off a springboard. (Don't try this at home.) His enemies in Pomerania jeered at him and called him, 'the flying squirrel'. But was he nuts?

Of course, in December 1903 Wilbur Wright made the first powered flight. His partner and brother, Orville Wright, later said, 'No flying machine will ever fly from New York to Paris.'

Which just goes to prove, 'Two Wrights do make a wrong.'

Radio

In 1897 our old friend Lord Kelvin said,

Radio has no future.

As for sending message by radio, he went on 'Radio is all very well but I'd rather send a message by a boy on a pony.'

Clever Kelvin.

Moon rockets

In 1906 Dr Lee de Forest invented the 'vacuum tube', which made TV possible. He also told us,

Man will never reach the moon no matter what scientists invent in the future.

Now, you may think Dr Lee was w-r-o-n-g but he must have been right because Lord Kelvin told us in the 1890s, 'Landing and moving around on the moon has so many serious problems for human beings that it may take science another 200 years to lick them.'

So we have to wait another 90 years before we can see a man (or woman) walk on the moon.

You may THINK you have seen pictures of American astronauts walking on the moon, but some very suspicious people say it NEVER HAPPENED! They believe the whole moon walk was filmed in a studio and the world was tricked.

Telephones

These useless inventions were rubbished over 100 years ago. In 1876 a report said…

This 'telephone' has too many faults to be taken seriously. The machine is of no use to us.

Talking films

Silent movies were popular from the 1900s to the late 1920s and then someone invented a way of letting the audience hear the actors speak and sing. H M Warner owned Warner Brothers film studios so he was an expert. He must have been right when he said,

'Who the hell wants to hear actors talk?'

NOTE: Lord Kelvin was dead by then, so he was not able to tell us that talking films were impossible anyway.

X-rays

X-rays were first used in 1895 by Wilhelm Rontgen. They have been a medical marvel for over 100 years, helping millions of people. So the final word goes to good old Lord Kelvin, who told us in 1895,

X-rays will prove to be a trick.

DREADFUL DAYS

Before you get out of bed you should check what day it is. Some days are worse than others – dreadful days in fact. On those days it's better to stay in bed.

Sneeze on a Sunday, your safety seek,
For the devil will have you the whole of the week.
Sneeze on Monday, sneeze for danger;
Sneeze on Tuesday, kiss a stranger;
Sneeze on Wednesday, get a letter;
Sneeze on Thursday, something better;
Sneeze on Friday, sneeze for sorrow;
Sneeze on Saturday, see your sweetheart tomorrow.

On the other hand…

Sunday is a good day to go to sea.
Monday is a good day to start something new in Ireland.
Tuesday is a good day to sow corn.
Wednesday is a good day to be a witch in Wales.
Thursday is a good day to christen a baby.
Friday is a good day to get married in Scotland.
Saturday is a good day to choose a wife.

People have some strange superstitions. You probably know the rhyme ...

Monday's child is fair of face.
Tuesday's child is full of grace.

But did you know there are some other silly superstitions about the days of the week? Cutting your nails, for example...

Cut your nails on a Monday, cut them for news.
Cut your nails on a Tuesday, a new pair of shoes.
Cut your nails on a Wednesday, cut them for health.
Cut your nails on a Thursday, cut them for wealth.
Cut your nails on a Friday, cut them for woe.
Cut your nails on a Saturday, a journey to go.
Cut your nails on a Sunday, you cut them for evil,
For all the next week you'll be ruled by the devil.

The toenail curse

As far back as AD 77, and throughout the 1500s and 1600s, we find this recipe:

> Take the clippings of the toenails and the
> fingernails of a sick person.
> Mix them up with wax ... then stick this wax,
> before sunrise, upon the door of another person
> you hate.
> Your enemy will then get the sickness.

— WHAT DAY DID THEY DIE ON? —

The Horrible Histories team have uncovered an amazing fact NEVER before noticed by a history writer: every single British monarch had died on a day that ends in 'y'!

Sunday	Henry I **Edward III** Henry VI **James I** William III **Edward VIII** Anne
Monday	Stephen **Henry IV** Henry V **Richard III** George V **Lady Jane Grey**
Tuesday	Richard I **Edward II** Charles I **James II** William IV **Victoria**
Wednesday	John **Henry III** Edward IV **George VI**
Thursday	William I **William II** Henry II **Edward VI** Mary I **Elizabeth I**
Friday	Edward I **Henry VIII** Charles II **Mary II** Edward VII
Saturday	Henry VII **George I** George II **George III** George IV **Richard II**

— DIRE DEATHS – BRITISH RULERS —

Here are some monarch mishaps you probably wouldn't want to suffer yourself…

Date of Death	Name	Cause of Death	
946	Edmund I (the Magnificent)	Stabbed by a robber at a feast in Pucklechurch, Gloucestershire	
978	Edward (the Martyr)	Hacked to death by his stepmother's servants	
997	Kenneth (of Scotland)	Arrows released from a booby-trapped statue	
1042	Harthacnut	Choked at a drunken wedding-feast in Lambeth	
1066	Harold II	Hacked to death by Normans at Battle of Hastings	
1087	William I	Burst gut after falling on the pommel of saddle	
1100	William II (Rufus)	New Forest hunting accident, when a hunter shot him with an arrow	
1135	Henry I	Food poisoning from eating too many lampreys (eels)	
1199	Richard I (Lionheart)	Gangrene following a wound at the siege of Châlus in France	
1327	Edward II	Murdered with a red-hot poker	
1437	James II (of Scotland)	An exploding cannon that he was standing next to during the siege of Roxburgh	

Date of Death	Name	Cause of Death	
1471	Henry VI	Murdered in the Tower of London after being knocked off the throne	
1483	Edward V	Imprisoned then murdered in Tower of London (aged 13)	
1485	Richard III	Killed at Battle of Bosworth	
1554	Lady Jane Grey	Beheaded	
1649	Charles I	Beheaded	
1702	William III	Fell from his horse when it stumbled over a molehill	

 # DIRE DISASTERS II

Of course, humans don't need nature to kill them. Humans are very good at killing themselves. Here are a few nasty accidents that have happened in history...

Flaming fires
19 July AD 64: Great Fire of Rome
• Started in shops near Circus Maximus. Burned for a total of nine days.

• Wiped out two-thirds of the city (population about two million).

• The people blamed Emperor Nero – Nero blamed Christians for it and began to massacre them.

1212: First Great Fire of London

• Fire killed up to 3,000 people. BUT…

22 September 1666: Great Fire of London

• Started in a baker's shop. Raged for four days. Destroyed four-fifths of London: 423 acres, 87 churches and 13,000 houses. Only six people died.

• The Londoners blamed their French enemies for starting it. A Frenchman owned up – he was hanged, even though he arrived in London three days after the fire started!

8 October 1871: Chicago fire

• Burned 17,450 buildings and killed 250 people; 90,000 people were made homeless.

• A maid was milking a cow by the light of an oil lamp. The cow kicked the lamp over into the straw and started the fire. Moo was to blame?

30 December 1903: Iroquois theatre fire, USA

During a sold-out afternoon show a spark from a faulty light set fire to the curtain. 600 people were killed.

Seasick

27 April 1865: Sultana steamboat disaster

• The boiler of a Mississippi River steamboat the *Sultana* explodes near Memphis.

• 1,547 were killed. Most were prisoners of war, returning home after the American Civil War.

15 April 1912: The sinking of the Titanic, in the Atlantic Ocean, off Newfoundland

• The 'Unsinkable' British luxury liner hits an iceberg and sinks.

• 1,500 were killed. But many women, children (and rich men) are saved. Oddly two dogs were saved from the ship.

• The *Titanic* was the first ship to use the SOS (Save Our Souls) signal. It became the signal for distress in 1912.

6 December 1917: The explosion of the Mont Blanc in Halifax Harbour, Nova Scotia

• After colliding with a steamer, the *Mont Blanc*, an ammunition ship carrying 2,500 tons of explosives blew up.

• Between 1,600 and 2,000 were killed; 9,000 were injured;

25,000 were made homeless; and 2 km² of Halifax was flattened.

• It was the largest explosion of the First World War. (And was the largest man-made explosion until the Americans dropped an atomic bomb on Hiroshima in 1945.)

30 January 1945: Sinking of the Wilhelm Gustloff in the Baltic Sea

• The *Wilhelm Gustloff* a ship carrying German refugees was sunk by a Russian submarine.

• 900 survived, but the ship may have been carrying up to 6,000.

• The German ship was going to be called the *Adolf Hitler,* but Hitler thought it would be unlucky – for him. Instead it was named after a dead Nazi hero.

6 March 1987: Herald of Free Enterprise ferry disaster, in the English Channel, near Zeebrugge, Belgium

• The bow doors were left open and water swept through the car deck of the ferry. The boat sank soon after leaving the harbour.

• 134 people died.

Big bang

15 January 1919: Great Boston treacle flood, Boston, USA

• Tank containing 2 million gallons of treacle exploded in Boston. A 2.44-m wave of molasses drowned 21 people.

6 May 1937: Hindenburg airship disaster, New Jersey, USA

• The luxury transatlantic airship exploded on landing.

• Filled with hydrogen gas, it burst into flames in seconds, killing 35 people.

18 March 1937: Fire in New London, Texas, USA

• A gas explosion in a school killed 294 children and teachers.

26 April 1942: Honkeiko Colliery, Manchuria (China)

• An explosion in a mine killed 1,549 people. It was the worst-ever mining disaster.

3 June 1989: Ural Mountains, near Moscow, Soviet Republic

• Petrol leaked from a pipeline next to the Trans-Siberian Railway.

• It exploded, destroying two passing passenger trains, and killing around 500 people.

Cruel crash

28 December 1879: Tay Bridge, Scotland

• A train was crossing the Tay Bridge in a storm when the bridge collapsed. Seventy-nine passengers were catapulted into the dark, icy waters of the Tay below. There were no survivors at all.

• The bridge was unsafe and the bridge inspector was questioned. It turned out that the bridge inspector had no idea about bridge building. He wouldn't have spotted a faulty bridge if it had fallen on his head.

Christmas Eve 1953: Whangaehu Bridge, New Zealand

• There is a lake in the crater of the Ruapehu volcano. When the volcano erupted, the lake water, rocks and lava spewed into the River Whangaehu. The river flooded and the rush of mud-thick water weakened the bridge.

• The weight of the train on the bridge caused it to collapse and the locomotive dragged the front carriages into the river.

• Passengers in the rear carriages bravely formed a human chain to pull survivors out. 131 people died and a further 20 people were never found. (The disaster was made worse by the train being crowded with people going home for Christmas.)

6 June 1981: Near Mansi, India
• A train driver braked to avoid hitting a cow (sacred animals for Hindus).
• The train plunged off the bridge and between 250 and 500 were killed.

Criminal crushes

AD 27: Collapse of stadium in Fidenae, near Rome
• The badly built stadium collapsed on 50,000 people.
• There were between 20,000 and 50,000 casualties. (Serves them right. They were going there to see criminals executed and people torn apart by wild animals.)

24 May 1964: Peru vs Argentina football match in Lima, Peru
• An unpopular decision by the referee caused a riot which killed 300 and injured 500. The worst football disaster in history.

2 July 1990: Fatal stampede in Mecca, Saudi Arabia
• Thousands of Muslim pilgrims in the Holy City of Mecca stampeded in a tunnel killing 1,400.

1996: Stampede at railway station in Johannesburg, South Africa
• Security guards at the railway station were paid to control the crowds, but they used electric cattle prods. The crush killed 15 people.

1789: Sadler's Wells Theatre, London

• Lady Luker was a hooligan and a drunk. When friends started arguing at Sadler's Wells Theatre she stood up and shouted, 'Fight! Fight!' Many thought she was shouting 'Fire!' and rushed to the doors. Eighteen people died in the crush.

THE VICTORIA HALL DISASTER – THE CRUELLEST CRUSH

Some disasters are sad because the victims are so young – and the accident could have been avoided. Take the Victoria Hall disaster in Sunderland, north-east England, in 1883.

The ticket promised drama and excitement…

Victoria Hall, Sunderland,
On Saturday Afternoon at 3 o'clock.

SCHOOL TICKET

THE FAYS

From the Tynemouth Aquarium,
Will give a Grand Day Performance for Children.
THE GREATEST TREAT FOR CHILDREN EVER GIVEN
Conjuring, Talking Waxworks, Living Marionettes, The Great Ghost Illusion, &c.

This Ticket will admit any number of Children on payment of
ONE PENNY Each; Reserved Seats, 2d., Nurses or Parents with Children 3d.

PRIZES!

Every child entering the room will stand a chance of receiving a handsome Present, Books, Toys, &c. This Entertainment has been witnessed by thousands of delighted Children throughout England.

But that 'greatest treat for children ever given' turned into the greatest nightmare and the greatest disaster ever for some Sunderland children.

On 16 June 1883 over 1,500 children flocked to see Mr Fay and his assistants perform their spectacular show. There weren't a lot of adults there to control them – not at three pence a ticket. They couldn't afford it. Most parents let their children go alone or with brothers and sisters.

Even little Georgina Coe from Wear Street hobbled along on her crutches. She found a seat near the door and joined in happily with the shouting and the singing. What a wonderful day out.

It started to go wrong when one of the tricks used a lot of smoke. Several children were sick and had to leave. They were the lucky ones.

The others choked a little but stayed on for those 'handsome presents' at the end. Of course the poster did NOT say every child WOULD get one. It only said every child would have the 'chance' of getting one.

And those 'handsome presents' were thrown into the audience that sat close to the stage. The children in the gallery upstairs soon realized they were going to miss out and headed for the stairway down. It was just over 2 metres wide and hundreds of children crushed into it, screaming, giggling, excited. Georgina Coe was one of the first ones there.

But when they reached the bottom of the stairs there were problems getting out. The door opened inwards, towards them, and there was so much pushing that a boy became jammed.

The door was fixed to open just half a metre wide so that only one child at a time could pass through. (That was to stop children slipping in without paying.)

As more children tumbled down the stairs they piled on top of the ones trapped at the bottom. Georgina Coe managed to wedge a crutch across her body to form a barrier, but the others were crushed under the weight of the avalanche of young bodies. The heap became 20 deep and 3 metres high.

An attendant managed to pull some out, one by one, through the half-metre gap. But many were already dead. One man cursed the owners of the theatre as he tore the locked door from its hinges.

It was too late for 187 children, who were already trampled under the weight of their friends, their brothers and their sisters. That awful afternoon 114 boys and 69 girls died. A further 100 were seriously injured. Most were between the ages of seven and ten. Dorothy Buglass and Margaret Thompson were just three years old.

Several families lost three children. The Mills family lost four.

One little girl was stopped as she walked away from Victoria Hall; she was carrying her dead sister home to their mother. A passer-by called a cab and paid for her to get home.

As news of the disaster spread through Sunderland the tormented parents rushed to the scene. Many fought with the rescuers to get inside, desperate to find their children.

Sunderland was in mourning. The funerals began the next day and went on for weeks.

And little Georgina? She lived. But what sort of nightmares haunted her dreams from that day on?

What is left today? Victoria Hall is gone. In time a memorial was built in Mowbray Park opposite the site. It showed a statue of a weeping mother clutching the body of her dead child.

The statue was damaged by vandals and was moved. For a long time it was forgotten, but it has been restored and is back where it belongs in Mowbray Park. A sad reminder of the 'greatest treat for children ever given'.

COOL FOR CATS

The Egyptians loved their cats. Worshipped them. Once, when an enemy invader threatened to kill their cats, the Egyptian army gave in. They couldn't bear to live without them.

In fact they loved them so much, the posh Egyptians couldn't bear to die without them. They had the cats mummified and put in their tombs with them. The cats would probably rather have had a dish of milk and a fish tail. But that's life ... and death.

Don't worry. Life hasn't always been that bad for cats. Here are ten feline facts...

1. Ancient Egyptians believed that the goddess Bast was the mother of all cats on earth. They also believed that cats were holy animals.

2. In ancient Egypt, the whole family would shave their eyebrows as a sign of sadness when the family cat died.

3. The punishment for killing a cat, 4,000 years ago in Egypt, was death.

4. 'Catgut' was once used as strings in tennis rackets and musical instruments. The Egyptians would be pleased to know it did not come from cats. Catgut actually comes from sheep, pigs and horses.

5. In the reign of Kublai Khan, the Chinese used lions on

hunting expeditions. They trained the big cats to chase and drag down large animals – from wild bulls to bears – and to stay with the kill until the hunter arrived.

6. The only common domestic animal not mentioned in the Bible is the cat.

7. The phrase 'raining cats and dogs' comes from England in the 1600s. During heavy downpours of rain, many of these poor animals drowned. Their bodies could be seen floating in the rain that raced through the streets. It looked as if it had rained 'cats and dogs'.

8. When a house cat goes after mice, about one pounce in three gets a catch.

9. When the Black Death swept across Europe, some people said that cats had caused the plague. Thousands were slaughtered. But the people who kept their cats were often saved – the cats kept their houses clear of the real villains, rats.

10. In 1888, about 300,000 mummified cats were found at Beni Hassan, Egypt. They were sold at $18.43 per ton, and shipped to England to be ground up and used for fertilizer.

Mysteries of the cat world... *WHY ISN'T THERE MOUSE-FLAVOURED CAT FOOD?*

A DOG'S LIFE

As for those cats' old enemies, dogs, they've had their place in history too.

1. The dachshund is one of the oldest dog breeds in history (going back to ancient Egypt). The name comes from one of its earliest uses – hunting badgers. In German 'dachs' means 'badger' and 'hund' means 'hound.' (Owners get upset if you call it a 'sausage dog' – daschunds have never been used to hunt sausages.)

2. Dogs are mentioned 14 times in the Bible.

CATS ARE HEATHEN, DOGS ARE HOLY

WHO DO YOU THINK GOT THE MICE OUT OF THE MANGER?

3. In the ancient Greek story *The Odyssey* the hero Odysseus arrived home after being away for ten years. (He had been fighting at Troy.) Because he was disguised as a beggar, the only one to recognize him was his old dog, Argos. The marvellous mutt wagged his tail at his master ... and then died.

4. Pekinese dogs were sacred to the emperors of China for more than 2,000 years. They are one of the oldest breeds of dogs in the world.

5. Greyhounds were bred in Egypt about 5,000 years ago. They came to England some time in the 800s. The Saxon lords used them to hunt hares.

6. French Queen Marie Antoinette's dog was a spaniel named Thisbe. But Thisbe was a character in Greek myths who died horribly with lots of blood. Not a nice name for the poor pooch. Marie-A lost her head on the guillotine – a horrible and bloody death. (This-be something you shouldn't try at home.)

7. In 1978 a law said New York City dog owners had to clean up after their pets. Before that about 40 million pounds (18 million kilos) of dog poo was left on the streets every year.

WE REALLY SHOULD DO SOMETHING ABOUT THIS

8. The last member of the famous Bonaparte family, Jerome Napoleon Bonaparte, died in 1945. He was fatally injured when he tripped over his dog's lead.

The great dog question... *WHY IS IT THAT WHEN YOU BLOW IN A DOG'S FACE HE GETS ANNOYED, BUT WHEN YOU TAKE HIM IN A CAR, HE STICKS HIS HEAD OUT OF THE WINDOW?*

SNIFF

Ten Torture Tools to Teach you to Talk

The top time for torturers was probably the Middle Ages and Tudor times. Here is a tortured top ten of their horrible habits and instruments.

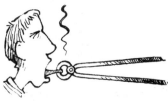

1 The red-hot pincers. They nip your flesh, or your tongue, off bit by bit. Are you feeling the pinch?

2 The press. The more stones that are piled on you the flatter you get. Chatter ... or flatter till splatter?

5 The boot. An iron boot with wedges to crush the ankle – tell or yell.

6 The brakes. A mask that has pincers to pull out your teeth one at a time – fangs a lot.

7 The gyves (scavenger's daughter). A hoop with a hinge Pop in and close the hoop. A hinge to make you whinge.

3 Thumbscrews. Won't talk? Pop this little machine on your thumbnails and tighten it slowly. You'll soon be saying thumb-thing.

4 The strappado. Just a rope and a beam to pull your arms from their sockets. Cough up or crack up?

OW!

10 The rack. If all else fails, the rack will stretch you till you crack.

9 The iron chair. Sitting comfortably? Till it heats up! Cringe and singe.

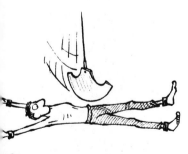

8 The pendulum. The blade swings closer and closer till you spit it out – or are split in two.

HISTORY MYSTERIES

You'd think that historians know everything. But they don't. They still argue about some of the strange happenings in the past. You decide which is the most likely...

1 The Princes in the Tower

King Richard III had his nephews locked up in the Tower of London, then took the throne of England for himself in 1483. A few months after Richard was crowned, the boys were never seen alive again – though many years later a couple of young skeletons were dug up. The skeletons could have been the Princes. What happened to them?

a) King Richard III gave orders to have them murdered and buried in the Tower.

b) The boys were sent away to live in hiding. Then (two years later) Richard III was killed in battle by Henry VII. It was Henry VII who found the Princes and had them murdered.

2 Prince Don Carlos

King Philip of Spain was a ruthless ruler but his son, Prince Don Carlos, was cruel and evil. Philip thought it would be a disaster for Spain if Don Carlos ever took the throne. He had his son locked away. Then one day, in 1568, Prince Carlos died. What killed him?

MY DARLING TWISTED BOY

a) King Philip had his son murdered – some say poisoned, some say he had him smothered, others that he had him beheaded or he was simply left to starve to death.

b) King Philip gave his son everything he wanted in his prison. But the greedy prince stuffed himself with partridge livers washed down with iced water. This gave him a chill and he died. Not murdered … but dead of his own gluttony.

3 King Tutankhamun

Three thousand years ago, in ancient Egypt, Tutankhamun died mysteriously when he was just 19 years old. A modern writer reckoned he was able to solve the mystery of the young King's death after studying X-rays of the mummy. Tutankhamun probably died from a blow to the head that fractured his skull. How did the healthy young King die?

a) The Prime Minister, a man called Ay, married Tutankhamun's widow and became the ruler of Egypt. He might have murdered Tutankhamun as he slept.

b) Tutankhamun slipped and fell, and died accidentally.

4 Prince Dimitry

In Russia, in 1591, Dimitry was a weedy youth. Would he be strong enough to rule a wild country like Russia when he grew up? Or would he be better off dead? It was said that he was playing with a knife in the courtyard of his mother's house when he had a fit. He cut himself and bled to death. A curious way to die! What happened to Dimitry?

a) Some people suspected he had been murdered – he was stabbed and left to bleed to death.

b) Some believed Dimitry had escaped and the corpse was another child.

c) But the mystery was just beginning, because 12 years later a young man turned up and claimed to be the dead Prince

Dimitry. People believed him and he took the throne. After a while there was a rebellion in which Dimitry II was hacked to pieces and died … again. Shortly afterwards a third Dimitry appeared and claimed the throne! He was murdered by a servant while he was out hunting. Third time lucky – and this time Dimitry III stayed dead!

5 Lord Darnley

Mary Queen of Scots was married to Lord Darnley. In 1567, while she was away from their home in Edinburgh, the house was blown up and Darnley was murdered. Who killed Darnley?

a) Most people were sure that Mary Queen of Scots arranged the murder. Mary's letters were found in a silver casket and they seemed to prove that she was guilty. But the letters have disappeared and we only have copies.

b) Darnley was killed by one of his many enemies. Mary was innocent and the letters were a forgery written by HER enemies.

6 Tsar Alexander I

In Russia, in 1825, Tsar Alexander was not happy being on the Russian throne. He wanted to retire. His own father had been brutally murdered, his favourite sister and his daughter had died of disease, and he was miserable. He went off to Taganrog, a small port on the Sea of Azov, for a holiday. The holiday was spoiled by the death of a messenger who smashed his skull in a coach accident. It was said that Tsar Alexander died of cholera (or, some say, a cold). Or did he?

NOT HAPPY

ME NEITHER

a) Tsar Alexander caught malaria and died.

b) The Tsar put the servant's body in the coffin and disappeared to retire the way he wanted to. Tsar Alexander's tomb was opened in the late 1880s and again in 1926. Both times it proved to be empty.

7 King Ludwig of Bavaria

In 1886 the 40-year-old King Ludwig of Bavaria was said to be mad so he was replaced on the throne by his uncle. Ludwig was sent to the castle of Berg on Lake Starnberg to be treated. The evening after he arrived he set off for a walk with his 62-year-old doctor. When they didn't return, a search was made and both men were found drowned at the edge of the lake. The doctor's hat had come off and it was battered. The King's coat and jacket were found by the edge of the lake. What happened?

a) In a fit of madness Ludwig had smashed the doctor over the head but failed to kill him. He threw off his top clothes and tried to swim away to safety. The doctor caught him and they both drowned in the struggle.

b) The doctor was ordered to kill Ludwig to keep the uncle on the throne. But the doctor got it wrong and was killed by Ludwig. Ludwig had then taken off his top clothes to swim across the lake and escape – or to kill himself.

 **SHAKESPEARE'S SLURS**

Of course, you can't go around insulting people and get away with it, but if you say these things with a smile, as if it's something nice, then you may just get away with it.

From the play: King Lear

'Thou art a boil, a plague sore, an embossed carbuncle in my corrupted blood.'

Troilus and Cressida

'Thou has no more brain than I have in mine elbows.'

'He has not so much brain as ear wax.'

Henry IV, Part 2

'I scorn you, scurvy companion. What, you poor, base, rascally, cheating, lack-linen mate!'

'Thou damned tripe visaged rascal.'

Henry IV, Part 1

'Peace, ye fat guts.'

'Out, you mad headed ape.'

'Why, thou clay-brained guts, thou knotty-pated fool, thou whoreson obscene greasy tallow-catch.'

Henry IV, Part 2

'Hang yourself, you muddy conger.'

'His wit's as thick as a Tewkesbury mustard.'

Henry VI, Part 2

'His breath stinks with eating toasted cheese.'

The Taming of the Shrew

'Away, you three inch fool.'

The Tempest
'What strange fish hath made his meal on thee.'

Timon of Athens
'Were I like thee I'd throw away myself.'
'Would thou were clean enough to spit on.'

The Merry Wives of Windsor
'You Banbury cheese.'
'Out of my door, you witch, you hag, you baggage,
you polecat, you ronyon fat old bag!'

King John
"Thou odoriferous stench."

Julius Caesar
'Where will thou find a cavern dark enough to mask
thy monstrous visage?'
"Base dunghill villain and mechanical."

Deadly Shakespeare insult...
From Measure for Measure
'Your bum is the greatest thing about you.'

Deadliest Shakespeare insult of all...
From King Lear
'Thou base football-player.'

AWFUL ABDICATIONS

Kings and queens are powerful people, but so many of them in history have been potty. Take Peter I of Portugal (1320–1367) who was also known as Pedro the Cruel. He married a maidservant, Ines de Castro, and his father had her murdered in 1355. Peter led two revolts against his deadly dad and took the throne. But he still wanted Ines to be his queen. So he had her dug up, dressed up, propped up and crowned.

Most monarchs rule until they die a natural death ... or until they are bumped off. But not all of them. Some give up their power and let another ruler take over. They 'abdicate'. Say, 'See you later abdicator!' to...

Sulla Roman Dictator
Abdicated: 79 BC
Reason: He'd had enough of ruling ruthlessly and murdering his enemies.
What happened: Retired to write his diaries (in 22 books).

Diocletian Roman Emperor
Abdicated: 305 BC
Reason: Illness.
What happened: Retired to his palace in Split (modern Croatia) to grow cabbages. He was asked to return as Emperor but said 'If people could only see one of the cabbages I've grown, they'd understand why I prefer gardening to being emperor.' (Could be that he had a cabbage for a brain.)

Richard II King of England
Abdicated: 1399
Reason: Captured on return from Ireland by Henry IV, who had made himself king. Richard gave up without a fight. It did him no good.
What happened: Imprisoned in Pontefract Castle and probably murdered there.

Charles V Holy Roman Emperor
Abdicated: 1556
Reason: Worn out/nervous breakdown.
What happened: Retired to a monastery.

Mary Queen of Scots Queen of Scotland
Abdicated: 1567
Reason: Unpopular, largely because of her Catholic beliefs and her villainous husbands.
What happened: Gave the throne to her one-year-old son, then fled to England. There she was imprisoned, then executed, by her cousin, Elizabeth I.

James II King of England
Abdicated: 1688
Reason: Forced off throne because he was a Catholic.
What happened: He fled to France and the British Parliament decided he had 'abdicated'.

Napoleon I Emperor of France
Abdicated: 1814
Reason: Defeated in battle at Leipzig in Germany.
What happened: Exiled to island of Elba. Returned to rule for a 100 days until finally defeated at Waterloo. Then exiled on St Helena.

King Louis Philippe King of France
Abdicated: 1848
Reason: Rebels decided they wanted rid of him and even Louis Philippe's army was on their side.
What happened: Louis was told to abdicate as he ate dinner. He was in such a hurry that he wrote out his abdication on the tablecloth.

Nicholas II Russian Tsar (Emperor)
Abdicated: 1917
Reason: Forced to abdicate during Russian Revolution, when Communist workers took over.
What happened: The following year he and his family were massacred by revolutionaries.

Wilhelm II German Emperor
Abdicated: 1918
Reason: Forced to abdicate after German defeat in World War I.
What happened: Fled to Holland to spend more time on his hobby ... archaeology.

Edward VIII British King
Abdicated: 1936
Reason: Wanted to marry a divorced American woman, Mrs Wallis Simpson, which was frowned upon by many people.
What happened: Married Mrs Simpson and retired to France.

LEFT-HANDED RULERS

Here's one of those truly useful lists – so now everyone will think you are a genius when you tell them what Julius Caesar and Queen Victoria had in common...

Ramses II
Egyptian Pharaoh
1320–1224 BC

Alexander the Great
King of Macedonia
356–323 BC

Julius Caesar
Roman Emperor
100–44 BC

Tiberius
Roman Emperor
42 BC–AD 37

Charlemagne
Holy Roman
Emperor
AD 742–814

Napoleon
Bonaparte
Emperor of France
1769–1821

Edward III
King of England
1312–1377

George II
King of England
1683–1760

Louis XVI
King of France
1754–1793

Queen Victoria
Queen of England
1819–1901

George VI
King of England
1895–1952

Fidel Castro
Cuban President
1926–

Elizabeth II
Queen of England
1926–

ROYAL NICKNAMES

Many people have nicknames and monarchs are no different. But would you like to be called 'Tracey the Terrible' or 'Michael the Mad'? Which of these would suit you?

Charles (II) the Bad	(King of Navarre, 1349–1387)
Charles (II) the Bald	(Holy Roman Emperor, 843–877)
Charles (II) the Lame	(King of Naples, 1285–1309)
Charles (III) the Simple	(King of France, 893–922)
Charles (V) the Wise	(King of France, 1364–1380)
Edward (III) the Confessor	(Anglo-Saxon King of England, 1042–1066)
Ethelred (II) the Unready	(Anglo-Saxon King of England, 978–1016)
Ivan (IV) the Terrible	(Tsar of Russia, 1547–1584)
Ivar the Boneless	(King of Dublin, 856–873)
Joanna the Mad	(Spanish Queen of Castile, 1505–1555)
John (I) the Dead	(King of France, 1316). Only lived for five days
John the Fearless	(Duke of Burgundy, 1404–1419)
Louis (II) the Stammerer	(Holy Roman Emperor, 846–879)
Louis (III) the Blind	(Holy Roman Emperor, 901–905)
Louis (V) the Do Nothing (or Louis the Sluggard)	(King of France, 979–987)
Louis (VI) the Fat	(King of France, 1108–1137)
Louis (X) the Quarrelsome (or Louis the Stubborn)	(King of France, 1314–1316)
Olaf the Stout (or Olaf the Fat)	(King of Norway, 1015–1028)
Pedro the Cruel	(King of Castile, 1350–1369)
Philip the Tall (or Philip the Long)	(King of France, 1316–1322)

Pippin (III) the Short	(King of the Franks, 751–768)
Ragnar (Lodbruk) Hairy Breeches	(King of Denmark and Sweden, c. 835–865)
Suliman (I) the Magnificent	(Ottoman Sultan, 1520–1566)
Thorfinn (I) the Skull-splitter	(Earl of Orkney, lived c. 890–977)
Vlad (III) the Impaler (or Vlad Dracula)	(Prince of Wallachia, 1456–1477)
William (I) the Conqueror	(King of England, 1066–1087)

ODD OLYMPICS

In 1896 the idea of a modern 'Olympic' Games began and they have been held every four years since then (except during World Wars).

The sports events have changed over time. In 1904 there was an event called 'plunging'. The swimmers had to dive in the pool and float as far as possible in a minute. Today you can get an Olympic medal for synchronized swimming.

But if you wanted a REAL Olympic Games, the way the ancient Greeks had them, then they'd be a bit different. For a start, the runners all raced with no clothes on – and women were banned even from watching. One woman who sneaked in, disguised as a trainer, was thrown off a cliff. 'Throwing-the-woman-off-the-cliff' was not an Olympic sport, of course...

So what sports DID the ancient Greeks have in their Olympics? And what were they like?

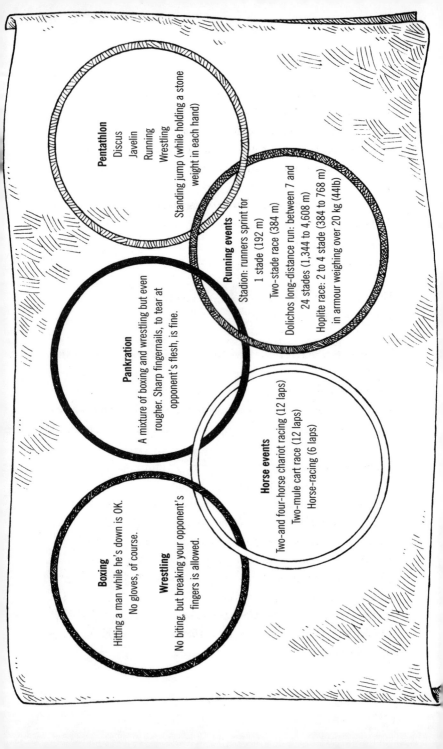

Pentathlon
Discus
Javelin
Running
Wrestling
Standing jump (while holding a stone weight in each hand)

Running events
Stadion: runners sprint for 1 stade (192 m)
Two-stade race (384 m)
Dolichos long-distance run: between 7 and 24 stades (1,344 to 4,608 m)
Hoplite race: 2 to 4 stade (384 to 768 m) in armour weighing over 20 kg (44lb)

Pankration
A mixture of boxing and wrestling but even rougher. Sharp fingernails, to tear at opponent's flesh, is fine.

Horse events
Two-and four-horse chariot racing (12 laps)
Two-mule cart race (12 laps)
Horse-racing (6 laps)

Boxing
Hitting a man while he's down is OK.
No gloves, of course.

Wrestling
No biting, but breaking your opponent's fingers is allowed.

Five ancient Greek athletic champions

Who were the stars of the Greek Olympics?

1 **Milo of Kroton** Wrestling champion in 532, 528, 524, 520 and 516 BC.
The most famous wrestling champion of ancient times. He is said to have eaten 20 kg (44 lb) of meat and potatoes in one sitting, washed down with 9 litres of wine.

2 **Theagenes of Thasos** Boxing champion in 480 BC and pankration champion in 476 BC.
After his death the people of Thasos built a statue in honour of Theagenes. One boxer had never been able to beat Theagenes, and after the champ's death the loser came every night to beat the statue instead (with a stick). But one night the statue fell on him and killed him. His sons took the statue to court for murder.

3 **Diagoras of Rhodes** Boxing champion in 464 BC.
A legend in his time, some claimed he was the son of Hermes, the messenger of the gods. Three of Diagoras's sons and two of his grandchildren went on to become Olympic champions.

4 **Polydamus of Skotoussa** Pankration champion in 408 BC.
Said to have killed a lion with his bare hands and beat three Persians in a three-against-one fight. Killed when a building collapsed and he was unable to hold the roof up.

5 **Melankomas of Caria** Boxing champion in AD 49.
Not beaten once in his entire career. His unusual style was to avoid the blows of his opponent and never to hit back! His opponents got so fed up that they gave up. He once trained by holding his arms up in the air for two days.

Not a lot of Olympic athletes know...

In the 1932 Olympics Stella Walsh of the USA beat Hilda Strike of Canada to take the 100 m gold medal.

In 1981 Stella Walsh was shot dead in the crossfire at a robbery in Ohio. Golden-girl Walsh turned out to be a man.

Yes, the women's 100 m was won by a man. As the headlines should have said...

STELLA WAS A FELLA!

The great athletes' question... *WHY IS IT THAT PEOPLE HAVE NOSES THAT RUN AND FEET THAT SMELL? ARE THEY BUILT UPSIDE DOWN?*

Not a lot of sports people know…

The world's 'greatest' goalkeeper was William 'Fatty' Foulke (1874–1916). This giant was 160 kg (25 stone) and played for Sheffield United, Chelsea and Bradford City. He…

• once got to the dinner table early and ate the food set out for the whole team. He then ate the food that was meant for the other side;

• picked up players from the other side if they upset him. One was dumped head first into the mud and another thrown into the net;

• ran into a goalpost and snapped it in two;

• could punch the ball from his goal to the halfway line;

• was injured once and it took six men to carry him off the field because there was no stretcher strong enough to hold him.

 **ROTTEN RITERS**

Writers are funny people. Imagine their weird lives, sitting at desks writing books when they could be doing something useful – like cleaning toilets, swimming the English Channel or robbing banks.

And some writers have been very odd people with odd habits.

Here are some of the strangest…

DYLAN THOMAS (1914–1953) (WELSH POET) Would often get drunk, get on his hands and knees, and bark like a dog. (Once, when he ran outside to bite a lamp-post, he chipped a tooth and gave up.) The first poem he ever published was not written by him – he stole it from a magazine, 'The Boys' Own Paper'.

PIETRO ARETINO (1492–1556) (ITALIAN POET) Went to a theatre in 1556 and laughed till he fell off his seat. He banged his head on the floor and died.

WILLIAM WORDSWORTH (1770–1850) (ENGLISH POET) Once papered a room entirely with newspapers. His most famous poem is 'Daffodils' and he often wrote about flowers – yet he had no sense of smell.

ALGERNON CHARLES SWINBURNE (1837–1909) (ENGLISH POET) Liked a laugh. But he upset his guests one day when he slid down the banisters of his house – completely naked.

GERARD DE NERVAL (1800–1855) (FRENCH POET) Kept a pet lobster that he took for walks on the end of a ribbon.

DANTE GABRIEL ROSSETTI (1828–1882) (ITALIAN POET) Collected a zoo full of pets including a zebra and an armadillo. He even thought of buying an elephant to squirt water at his windows to clean them.

LORD TENNYSON (1809–1892) (ENGLISH POET) Spent his childhood lying in a churchyard among the graves. Creepy.

VIRGIL (70–19 BC) (ROMAN POET) Was really upset when his favourite pet fly died and he had a huge funeral for it. He could have written a great poem, couldn't he? 'My fly die, why? Sigh oh my, cry bye-bye.'

LI PO (701–762 BC) (CHINESE POET) Leaned over the side of a boat to kiss the reflection of the moon. He fell in the water and died. That's a wet thing to do.

LORD BYRON (1788–1824) (ENGLISH POET) Kept a pet bear. It's said that he also drank wine from a human skull. (If you don't think that's weird, maybe you should be a poet.)

LEWIS CARROLL (1832–1898) (ENGLISH WRITER) Author of Alice in Wonderland. Wrote his books standing up.

JEREMY BENTHAM (1748–1832) (ENGLISH WRITER) Author of 'An Introduction to the Principles of Morals and Legislation'. Had a curious pet – a teapot. His preserved body can still be seen in the South Cloisters of University College London.

PERCY BYSSHE SHELLEY (1792–1822) (ENGLISH POET) Wrote 'To the Skylark'. It seems the skylark never wrote back. He hated cats and once tied a moggy to a kite and set it up in a thunderstorm, hoping it would be struck by lightning. The cat lived and Percy had invented Kit-e-kite. (Shelley's wife had her husband's heart mummified when he died and she carried it everywhere. Not just poets are peculiar.)

DANTE GABRIEL ROSSETTI (1828–1882) (ITALIAN POET) When his wife killed herself he was so upset that he had all his poems buried with her. Seven years later he changed his mind and had them dug up and disinfected. They were then published.

CICERO (106–43 BC) (ROMAN WRITER) Made the mistake of writing nasty things about Roman leader Mark Anthony. Cicero's head was cut off and put on show. His hands were also lopped off to show people what happened to hands that wrote anything against Mark Anthony.

Book cell-ers

Lots of writers should be locked up. Sadly only a few ever are. Here are some of them:

Writer	Work	Crime
Thomas Paine (1737–1809)	English-American writer of *The Rights of Man*	Wanted to save King Louis from the guillotine in the French Revolution.
Jean Genet (1910–1986)	French playwright	Thief and pickpocket from the age of ten. Just escaped a life sentence.
Robert Leighton (1611–1684)	Scottish writer	Was whipped, had his ears cut off, his nose slit and was branded for writing against the Church.
O. Henry (1862–1910)	American short-story writer	Worked in a bank and some of the bank's money ended up in his own pocket.
Sir Thomas Malory (d.1471)	English poet who wrote *The Legends of King Arthur*	Locked away for being an armed robber, poacher and murderer.
François Villon (1431 – after 1463)	French poet	Killed a priest. Set free by King Louis XI as a coronation treat. Vicious Villon killed again, was banished ... and was never heard of again.
Fyodor Dostoevsky (1828–1910)	Russian writer and philosopher	Convicted of conspiracy against the tsar. While in front of a firing squad he was reprieved and sent to a labour camp in Siberia.

 # WISE LAST WORDS

If you are going to die, you may as well say something that will help people to remember you. The Mexican rebel Pancho Villa (1878–1923) lay dying and panicked because he couldn't think of anything! So his last words were ... 'Don't let it end like this. Tell them I said something.'

What sort of something? Here are a few top tips from Horrible Histories to help you get your last words perfect:

Rule 1 Try to get it right.
Writer H G Wells (1866–1946) was just as bad when he said...

Go away. I'm all right.

All wrong, more like.

Playwright Noel Coward, (1899–1973) said...

Goodnight, my darlings, I'll see you tomorrow.

Duh, wrong again.

Rule 2 Don't be a bad loser. Go with a smile, not a sour snap, as writer Lytton Strachey (1880–1932) did when he snarled...

If this is dying, I don't think much of it.

And US president Franklin D Roosevelt, (1882–1945) was no better when he groaned…

> I have a terrific headache.

President Charles de Gaulle of France (1890–1970) muttered…

> It hurts!

Rule 3 Even better, try to say something brave. Saint Lawrence was being burned to death in AD 258 and is believed to have said…

> Turn me, I am roasted on one side.

When the French revolutionary leader Georges Danton (1759–1794) went to the guillotine he said to the executioner…

> Show my head to the people. It's worth seeing.

Rule 4 Say something that suits you. Nostrodamus (1503–1566) was a prophet – he was supposed to look into the future. So his last words were…

> Tomorrow I shall no longer be here.

Spot-on! And the German composer Ludwig van Beethoven (1770–1827) was deaf so he joked…

> I shall hear in heaven!.

Rule 5 Try to say something 'noble' – especially if you are dying for your country. American rebel Nathan Hale (1755–1776) was about to be hanged by the British and said…

I am only sorry that I have just one life to lose for my country.

English General Lord Horatio Nelson (1758–1805), shot and dying at the Battle of Trafalgar, managed to say…

Thank God, I have done my duty.

(Some people reckon he turned to one of his captains and said, 'Kiss me, Hardy,' but who knows?)

Rule 6 Try to say something funny and people will remember the words – and remember you (maybe). The poet Heinrich Heine (1797–1856) said…

God will forgive me. It's his job.

We don't know God's reply, but Heinrich probably soon found out.

Worst last words

In 1813 General William Erskine, a useless soldier, jumped from a window in Lisbon. As he lay dying he looked up at the people around him and asked…

Now why did I do that?

He died before they could answer, 'Dunno, mate. You tell us.'

GRAVE TALK

Once you are dead there're no more last words to be said … but they can be written. On your tombstone. Throughout history people have written last words of wit and wisdom in stone. They are called 'epitaphs'. Here are a few for you to think about.

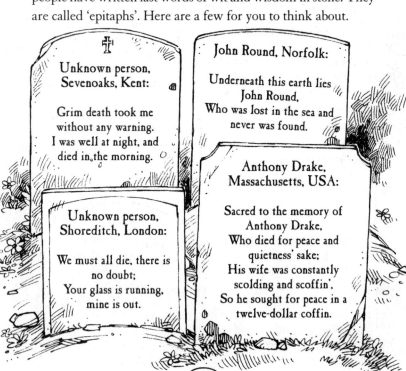

Unknown person, Sevenoaks, Kent:

Grim death took me without any warning. I was well at night, and died in the morning.

John Round, Norfolk:

Underneath this earth lies John Round, Who was lost in the sea and never was found.

Unknown person, Shoreditch, London:

We must all die, there is no doubt; Your glass is running, mine is out.

Anthony Drake, Massachusetts, USA:

Sacred to the memory of Anthony Drake, Who died for peace and quietness' sake; His wife was constantly scolding and scoffin', So he sought for peace in a twelve-dollar coffin.

William Shakespeare, Stratford-upon-Avon:

Good friend, for Jesus's sake
forbeare
To dig the dust enclosed here;
Blessed be he that spares
these stones,
And curst be he that moves
my bones.

Unknown person, Pembrokeshire:

Here I lie, and no wonder
I'm dead,
For the wheel of the wagon
went over my head.

John MacPherson:

John MacPherson was a
remarkable person
He stood 6 foot 2 without
his shoe,
And he was slew at Waterloo.

Infant, eight months old:

Since I have been so quickly
done for,
I wonder what I was begun for.

Joseph Jones, Wolverhampton:

Here lies the bones,
of Joseph Jones,
Who ate whilst he was able;
But once o'erfed, he drop't
down dead
And fell beneath the table.

Infant, Iowa, USA:

Beneath this stone our baby lays
He neither cries nor hollers.
He lived just one and twenty
days,
And cost us forty dollars.

Ann Mann, Bath Abbey:

Here lies Ann Mann;
She lived an old Maid and
she died an old Mann.

Martha Snell:

Poor Martha Snell! Her's
gone away,
Her would if her could, but
her couldn't stay;
Her'd two sore legs and a
baddish cough,
But her legs it was as carried
her off.

Robert Burrows, Bedlington, Durham:

Poems and epitaphs are but
stuff:
Here lies Robert Burrows,
that's enough.

DISCLAIMER

Where there's a fact there's an argument. There ARE some things in this book that people don't agree with[15]. Here are some of them:

1 The assassination of King Edmund in 1016 (page 22). Some people say there was not an assassin hiding under the toilet seat. Instead there was a crossbow, set to go off when the King sat down for a poo. But that seems to be a lot of trouble when a quick stab does the trick. Who knows? (Poo knows.)

2 Puppidog water (page 33). This recipe was published in the early 1700s listing some of the things women could do to make themselves look more beautiful. But it was meant as a huge joke. No one really did it. (Some history books have repeated it as if it was serious!) I only hope you didn't dash out and mash a nine-day-old puppy. You did? Oooops!

3 William II's death (page 96). Shot with an arrow while out hunting. An accident? Some historians say it was murder. The man who shot him was an expert shot and not likely to make a mistake. And William was a rotten ruler. Even if he'd lived, he'd be dead by now so what does it matter?

4 Edward II's death (page 96). Most people believe he was murdered and his mangled body was shown to the people of England to prove it. But some people think he was allowed to escape and live in secret. The corpse belonged to some other

15. If you think any facts in this book are wrong then don't write to the author. He's too busy with the next-book-but-one to answer you. Anyway, he'll only tell you to blame the researchers. He will then sack the researchers and they will starve and you will feel really guilty.

poor bloke, dead instead of Ed. It's terrible when you can't even trust a murderer to be honest.

5 The Princes in the Tower, 1483 (page 112). Historians have argued for years about what happened to the Princes in the Tower. There is even a society set up to prove King Richard III is innocent of their murder. Horrible Historians know that Richard is guilty.

6 Lord Nelson's last words (page 133). Some say he didn't croak, 'Kiss me, Hardy!'. They say his words were 'Kismet, Hardy.' Now 'Kismet' means 'fate'. So his last words were, 'That's the way it goes, Hardy.' Maybe, if you die before me and get to meet Lord Nelson, you could ask him? Let me know what he says.

Most famous last words of all…

THE END

INTERESTING INDEX

What you need now is a boring old index. Well, tough. You are not going to get one. This is a Horrible Histories book so you can have an Interesting Index or nothing.

If you think it's a load of 'poo' (32, 52, 64, 109) then have the 'guts' (7, 33, 47, 49, 116) to ask for your money back, 'witch' (69, 117) we will pay you in 'goat droppings' (50).